NON-Food Franchising

The Better Path to Business Ownership

JON OSTENSON, CFC

Aragon House Publishing

Non-Food Franchising: The Better Path to Business Ownership
Copyright © 2022 by Jon Ostenson

ISBN (paperback) 979-8-9867430-0-4
ISBN (ebook) 979-8-9867430-1-1
ISBN (audiobook) 979-8-9867430-2-8

Cover design by Aaxel Author Services & Deividas Jablonskis
Interior design by Aaxel Author Services
www.aaxelauthorservices.com

Printed in the United States of America

This book is dedicated to my incredible clients whose consistent successes have inspired me to impact the lives of many more!

100% of profits from this book will be donated to Hope International, a Christian non-profit that supports entrepreneurs in underserved communities around the world through avenues such as microfinance loans and savings groups. Their 'hand-up vs. hand-out' approach empowers sustainable commerce that has an exponential impact on the entrepreneurs' families and communities for years to come.

CONTENTS

BUSINESS OWNERSHIP:
THE AMERICAN DREAM

"If you don't build your own dream, someone will hire you to help build theirs."
- Tony Gaskins

I believe that there is an entrepreneurial spirit inside each of us. Some act on it, some contemplate it, and some ignore it. But it still exists. Every day, I talk with those interested in exploring business ownership across the United States and Canada. As I do so, I pick up on commonalities, themes and trends.

To launch a business, you can start from scratch with a few dollars and an idea. You can build anything from an application for mobile phones to an automobile, invent anything from a service that others never thought of to constructing a better mousetrap. You can also purchase a business. There are several ways to do this. For instance, some entrepreneurs purchase struggling businesses with the aim of turning them around. But not everyone is interested in taking on the stress of righting a potentially sinking ship. Some entrepreneurs want a proven concept with proven systems. While there is no guarantee for success, there are plenty of ways to mitigate risks.

One of America's greatest entrepreneurial ideas throughout recent decades is the concept of a franchise. While it isn't quite accurate to say that Americans invented franchising, there is no question that

American companies were the first to perfect the framework. In fast food, some of the earliest chains date to the 1920s, including Howard Johnson (now better known now as a hotel) and White Castle. Of course, McDonald's is the world's largest franchisor, with over 36,000 outlets worldwide.

However, the focus of this book is on 'non-food' franchises. It may surprise you to learn that non-food franchising actually predates the fast-food chain concept. The Singer Company actually began franchising in 1851, offering others the opportunity to sell sewing machines. Imagine a time before most of our clothing was stitched overseas; in fact, even before the stitching and hemming of clothes was done in factories at all. In the 1800s, nearly every household had to sew their own clothes. Singer is often cited as the first real franchisor in American history - 70 years before any fast-food chains popped up.

In 1902, Rexall, a chain of pharmacies, came on the scene and created a pattern and framework that others then followed. And now, fast forward, times have certainly changed. Today, there are several thousand non-food franchise opportunities from which to choose. And, as you can imagine, the possibilities are staggering!

While many people are excited by the wealth of opportunities that exist, few know where to start. You may have asked yourself these types of questions in the past:

"Do I have what it takes?"

"What are the risks?"

"What are the potential rewards? Do they outweigh the potential concerns that may linger?"

Most people know someone, a friend or family member who has been highly successful in building a business of their own; many of us also know of someone for whom the entrepreneurial game 'didn't work out'. They went for the dream, like gold miners headed west in a Conestoga with the sign "California or Bust" and ended up ... busted.

Everyone's own experience comes into play in how they view the world, and in turn, how they think about their jobs, careers, and investments. If you've seen people who went bust, perhaps you've gotten cold feet, even though you have the desire and drive. It's also common for cautious relatives to tell you to 'get a job' or 'find steady work'.

But people with a positive, can-do mindset enjoy the process of thinking 'what if'? They will sprint, then jog, then walk, then tiptoe their way up to the edge of the diving board. Some will take the plunge. And after some time, the majority of those will ask themselves... 'why didn't I jump sooner'?

Paraphrasing Tony Gaskins, you can either support someone else's dreams or you can apply the same energy toward accomplishing your own. You can either get compensated for helping someone else build their empire, or you can build your own. Perhaps getting hired to build someone else's empire is the right thing for you or the right thing for this season in your life. There is certainly nothing wrong with being an employee. However, if something about that feels a little off to you, you're in the right place. You have the liberty to follow your own dream and chart your own path. After all, you only live once!

Often, people see business ownership as risky. However, consider an airplane pilot. The pilot has more control over outcomes when they are the ones flying the plane as opposed to when they are sitting in coach or even business class... I have seen so many people who have been asked to step off the airplane, often unexpectedly, sometimes just a few years before they're ready to retire, when there are few options for getting re-hired. Unless their contractual position provides a golden parachute, they will find their livelihood in free-fall.

They may realize too late that they have no control over decisions being made by 'the boss' or 'the ivory tower'... Serving at someone else's prerogative can be far riskier, no matter how loyal an employee you may be. To be non-expendable, you have to be the owner.

At this time in history, I believe that Americans should feel encouraged at our long-term prospects, regardless of the 24/7 news cycle's often discouraging headlines. What I see in my daily discussions with clients is a level of interest in business ownership that I personally believe to be unprecedented, and this should bode well for the future of our nation. People inherently WANT to own businesses. Whether it is the freedom that can be afforded by this path, the ability to control one's own destiny, or just a piece of the greater American dream, more and more are waking up to this inner desire.

Even prior to the global Covid pandemic, Americans were showing increased levels of interest in ownership for a number of reasons. Two of these are well articulated by Adam Grant:

'Burnout is being overwhelmed by work. Boreout is being underwhelmed by work.' Another way to say this is that having too much to do is exhausting, but having too little to do is demoralizing.

What did the global COVID pandemic do? Did it make people more cautious about opening a franchise? Not in the least. Since 2020, the interest level has accelerated - big time. People had the opportunity during the pandemic to slow down and question the path they were on. Maybe you're one of those who is wondering if it's too late to make a shift in what is now known as the Great Resignation, or as I refer to it, the 'Great Reassessment'? The answer is NO! It is not too late.

Now is the time to scratch that entrepreneurial itch!

Not only are people looking toward their future, imagining how they can live the life they have dreamed, they are also taking a keen interest in investing. In total as a country, we have record levels of cash sitting on the sideline. The stock market is as unpredictable as ever; crypto is even more volatile than usual, and many precious metals are flat. Interest rates will likely continue to be at lower historical levels in the coming years, despite rising from the levels seen in the age of COVID. We all recognize that, with institutional buying and the lower interest rates, there are also only so many good real estate deals to be had. So, where do you put your money to work? Have you ever considered that franchise ownership could be an investment opportunity instead of a 'job'?

Where is this interest coming from? The demographics range across all working age groups from people in their early twenties to late sixties. That being said, the most interest in non-food franchises has come from those in their thirties to fifties. However, we have done a solid handful of deals in the recent past for entrepreneurs in their twenties - and they are all killing it now! I love to imagine what their businesses will look like in the years ahead. You're never too old... nor too young to own a franchise.

Now, you might wonder if it is necessary to quit your job if you want to launch a franchise. The answer is 'No'. If you like the security of employment and want to test the waters before jumping in 100%, there are many options.

Roughly half of those we work with are stepping in full time as owner-operators, leaving their current jobs. The other half are looking to go 'semi-absentee' or 'semi-passive' with what we often refer to as an 'executive model'. This is a structure in which they keep their full-time job and hire a General Manager to run the day to day operations of their franchise investment. We will discuss this approach further in the pages that follow. For now, I hope it is encouraging to know that you can be successful either way.

We have shared that interest in business ownership is high—perhaps higher than ever before. So, what type of business should you get into, and under what general framework does it fall? What is best for you? To purchase an existing business, to build a startup from the ground, or purchase the rights to a proven model that comes with a playbook, ongoing support, and quite a few other benefits? We will cover these topics in detail in the chapters to follow.

'Franchising as an asset class'

Were you aware that you can use a franchise investment as part of your retirement portfolio? Many investors are seeing the potential returns and recognizing that the phrase I have coined - 'Franchising as an asset class' - can serve to diversify their wealth, making business ownership a piece of their total pie. We will discuss further throughout this book, as well.

The Trifecta

If you're considering joining the Great Reassessment, it's important to understand that there are benefits to business ownership beyond simply replacing employment income with business cash flow. You need to remember that you are also building an asset with exit value.

On top of that, you are able to write off expenses as a business owner that you cannot as a W-2 employee.

I like to call the three-pronged benefits of cash flow, asset appreciation, and expense tax write-offs the 'trifecta of business ownership'. Beyond the financial benefits that make up this trifecta, there also lies the potential for freedom, independence, and satisfaction in building something that others cannot take away from you. It goes without saying that, while the 'trifecta' provides tangible ownership benefits, there also exist other intangible ownership benefits.

More and more investors are waking up to the idea that franchising can truly be the better path to business ownership. Not interested in owning a place that focuses on flipping burgers or deep-frying chicken? Don't worry. There are countless opportunities outside of food when it comes to franchising.

FRANCHISING VS. STARTUPS

"I believe it is true that the difference between great people and everyone else is that great people create their lives actively, while everyone else is created by their lives, passively waiting to see where life takes them next."

- Michael Gerber

F ranchising isn't right for everybody. But for the vast majority of would-be business owners and investors, I firmly believe it is simply a better path.

In this chapter, we will explore the pros and cons of franchising. First, let's start with some basic considerations.

1. One of the top considerations for determining whether or not franchising is right for you is your personality profile. I have noticed that if someone is 'too entrepreneurial', thrives on constantly changing things up, and can't live within a framework or follow a playbook, franchising may not be right for them.

How can you be "too" entrepreneurial? Ask yourself: Do I insist on always reinventing the wheel? Some people are bored by running a system, while the genius of franchising is in the development of a system that works.

An entrepreneur that is focused on execution rather than tinkering too much will do very well in a franchise system. In my experience on the franchisor side of the house, I consistently observed that our top performers in the system were almost always those adhering most closely to the playbook.

Think of it like owning a car. Some car owners trick out their ride with all kinds of features. They love to go to the auto parts store, exploring all types of after-market add-ons and they typically do the work themselves. Other gear-heads go further, swapping out the entire engine, chopping the chassis to change the length of the car from bumper to bumper, molding different parts for the body to shape a one-of-a-kind hot-rod. Meanwhile, most car owners are happy to turn the key and drive their car down the road, trusting the design work to the manufacturer, and using the vehicle as a tool to get from point A to point B.

Franchising is set up to be a turnkey solution. If you're going to be tempted to "chop the chassis" in your business and turn it into something unique, franchising may not be the best option for you. It's just not a personality fit. But if you're into accelerating your career trajectory and getting from point A to B, franchising could be the ticket. After all, you are still a driver rather than a corporate 'passenger'.

2. As a franchise owner, you typically send 5-7% of your top-line revenue back to the franchisor in the form of a royalty. For the first 2 or 3 days a month (assuming your business grosses about the same amount daily), every penny that comes in goes to the franchisor. However, considering all of the systems you are getting, along with the marketing and operations support, this can actually be a great deal. If you were building from scratch, learning lessons the hard way vs. executing on best practices derived from prior lessons learned, the expenses tallied up may total a full week of revenue every month. It is all about perspective.

That being said, it is very important to ensure that you are getting a level of support from your franchisor that justifies the ongoing royalty. It needs to equate to an investment in the business, rather than a required expense. Not every franchisor's offering is as strong, nor is every system as tight as the next.

The percentage isn't the issue here. The goal is finding the right franchisor that delivers truly excellent value in return for your ongoing royalty investment.

3. Success rates of startups: According to The Small Business Administration (SBA), which defines a "small" business as one with 500 employees or less, in 2019, the failure rate of startups was around 90% over time. Research concludes that roughly 22% of startups fail in the first year, while 30% fail by the end of the second year, 50% by the fifth year, and 70% have disappeared before the end of their 10th year.

According to the U.S. Bureau of Labor Statistics in a recent entrepreneurship report, "It's generally accepted, because of their established, proven business practices, that franchises have higher success rates than independent businesses." This doesn't mean that buying a franchise is a guaranteed success, but it does suggest that franchise ownership is one way to significantly improve the viability of a long-term successful business. The same report states that "About 20 percent of all businesses in the U.S. close after the first two years of operation and a little over 38 percent after four years."

Note that the SBA and the Bureau of Labor Statistics may be using different research, but their findings are eerily similar. Want to run a startup? The odds are about 50/50 that your business will still be around in five years.

On the other hand, according to a five-year study performed by the franchise consulting firm FranNet, 92 percent of franchises launched were still in business after two years and 85 percent after five years. So why do franchises not only stay in business longer but often produce better profitability, oftentimes, earlier to launch? Based on my experience as a franchisor, a multi-brand franchisee, and a franchise consultant, here are my top 10 reasons.

Top Ten Reasons to Purchase a Franchise

1. Franchise owners 'start on 3rd base instead of on 1st base'. What baseball manager wouldn't prefer a triple to a single with their leadoff hitter? The odds of scoring a run during that inning are increased substantially. On day one as a franchise owner, you know the roadmap to profitability and can begin executing on it... With a startup, you'll have to determine if the business can even become profitable. You can do market research, but it may be difficult to know for sure without a great deal of trial and error. In many cases, it only takes one or two major errors to sink a startup!

2. Franchise owners know that their 'product market fit' has already been established. There is a known market willing to pay for the service or product you are providing... and you can build the business from early on in a way to achieve strong long-term profits based on this knowledge.

3. Proven playbooks are provided by the franchisor in areas such as marketing and operations. Running a business requires a broad variety of skills. If you're not already an expert in certain areas, this can present an issue for traditional startups. Imagine starting a business without a keen understanding of marketing - especially marketing in your selected industry. As a franchise owner, you are handed a proven, turnkey marketing system.

4. In addition to a marketing system inclusive of digital, print, media, etc, most franchisors have experienced team members and preferred vendors that have learned their business and accumulated large data sets from which to fine tune and optimize your marketing campaigns. Don't underestimate the value of getting more bang out of your marketing buck.

5. Franchise owners can step into a technology stack from the franchisor that has been previously selected and customized

for their needs. The heavy lifting has been done and you have one less thing to think about. Often, this technology may include internal development and systems as well as best in class 3rd party software customized to the particular franchise system.

6. With franchising, you have a mentor or 'coach' on the sidelines in the franchisor - you're not in this alone! To be cliche, you are in business for yourself, but not by yourself. The franchisor has a full support team of 'assistant coaches' whose purpose is helping you drive your business.

7. An often-overlooked benefit of franchising is that you will have the opportunity to exchange best practices and learnings with other owners across the country that are living parallel day to day lives as you. The areas for information exchange can include items such as the testing of different marketing vehicles, which pools are best to fish in to find great employees, and how to find and network with potential referral partner types in your local market. You are in alignment with these other franchisees, whose businesses increase in value as yours increases.

8. Ever since Rexall pharmacies began in 1902, franchise owners have benefitted from the collective buying power of a franchise system - whether it be for products, equipment, or services. This can be a massive value-add depending on the nature of the business - and it can often justify much of the royalty investment.

9. While it does not completely de-risk the franchise opportunity, having the opportunity to speak with other franchise owners through the 'validation process' (see Chapter 8 on the 'process') when exploring the franchise, plus having the benefit of being able to review the Item 19 of the franchisor's Franchise Disclosure Document (FDD) (see chapter 7 on

'legal') provides a franchise candidate with incredible insight into the financial potential of the business prior to making their purchase decision. By contrast, with a startup you are often drawing pro formas on the back of napkins and spit balling assumptions on revenues, expenses, ramp-up timeline, and so forth.

10. Finally, it is important to note that franchise businesses enjoy a 50% higher exit value, on average, compared to their non-franchise counterparts in like-kind industries. The Rinker School of Business recently conducted a study looking at over 2000 business sales over a ten-year period and across a wide variety of industries and found that franchise businesses traded, on average, at a 1.5X multiple of their non-franchise counterparts in the same industry. This is eye opening for many!

FRANCHISING VS. 'ENTREPRENEURSHIP THROUGH ACQUISITION'

"For the investor, a too-high purchase price for the stock of an excellent company can undo the effects of a subsequent decade of favorable business developments"
- Warren Buffett

I n this chapter, we will examine the pros and cons of franchising vs. purchasing an existing business.

Many of my clients are considering the purchase of an existing business and find themselves weighing the tradeoffs of that path against the pros and cons of the franchise route. There is a popular idea in entrepreneur/investor circles these days that the best way to get into business ownership is through buying into an existing operating business, whether it be a franchise or non-franchise resale. This approach of purchasing a business is often referred to as entrepreneurship through acquisition, or 'ETA'. More often than not, I have clients reach out after exploring a number of resale options, and after we consult together, the majority of these clients end up going with the franchise model instead.

There are several attractive aspects of ETA on the surface: the new business owner often has positive cash flow on day one. They acquire existing customers. They have market awareness due to the company's prior marketing efforts. Employees are likely already in place, equipment is (hopefully) working, and things are generally set up. The business is a known entity, at least to some extent, and there is a track record.

Caveat emptor: But let the buyer beware! What worked for previous owners in the past might not work as well in the future for a variety of reasons. There can be drawbacks to the ETA model. Usually, you will pay two to five times the existing annual earnings to acquire the business (and sometimes higher depending on the industry and other factors). In most cases, this means you won't recapture the purchase price for several years. To do so faster will require some combination of an increase in gross revenue, and/or a decrease in spending that does not negatively impact revenue, resulting in overall improvement of the bottom line.

This leads us to a second concern. Can you trust the bottom-line figures provided by the seller in the first place? I have found that the seller's financial books and records from which the projections are made most often require numerous caveats and add-backs, to the point that you are trusting the seller's iffy explanations and rosy expectations more often than hard, repeatable data.

Third, what about your human resources? If there's one thing most people don't like, it is change. Inheriting an existing team of employees, no matter how good they are individually and as a team, means there is a culture and a way of doing things that will be shaken up. Even in the best-case scenario, when all the employees are top notch, it is not always easy to get buy-in and retain the top talent. The seller may have no idea that half his team is already contemplating a move; they aren't likely to tell the owner that they're considering changing jobs, let alone thinking about switching careers, or even considering purchasing a franchise themselves!

In the worst-case scenario, you purchase a business and find that there are some dead-weight employees who need to be replaced immediately, only to discover that some of those people don't go quietly into the sunset. They can walk out with trade secrets, details, important documents or customer relationships. Even if they have a non-compete agreement, if they decide to break it, you may be in for a long legal battle that wasn't in your financial plan. In many states, non-competes are not even highly enforceable - or at least not worth pursuing legally. The exiting employees can also generate collateral damage through adding additional layers of change and anxiety amongst their former colleagues that plan to stick around (or at least for the time being). In short, inheriting people has as many unique possible pitfalls as there are advantages. Even the best, most reliable, irreplaceable employee is likely to feel some degree of inner anxiousness when a business changes hands. I don't mean to paint an overly cloudy picture, but I want to be realistic. Change is usually tough.

Next, what about brand awareness in the marketplace? That's a pro, right? Not necessarily. Brand awareness in the market may not always be a good thing - you are inheriting all the past experiences of customers, both positive and negative. You may have to rebrand to convince people that your business can be trusted. If you've ever seen that sign in a window that says "now under new management" you know that someone out there is trying to tell the customers that their experience is about to improve. But a sign in a window isn't worth much if people have stopped parking in the lot in the first place. An advertising campaign may be warranted.

Also, what seller is able (and willing) to tell you all about the customers that will likely quit coming? How many of the customers were loyal to the seller and may drop off? Rarely do they even get feedback on why people don't come back; the customer just ghosts. This means that the previous business owner has a blind spot; it isn't that they're being dishonest, it's just that they might not even know themselves. Maybe their customer base is dwindling because they're aging out, dying, going out of business themselves, irritated at something small, found a better deal elsewhere, didn't like the sales rep... the list goes on. Think about the businesses you have personally stopped patronizing. An auto mechanic, a grocery store, the local gym... Why? How many of them noticed when you left? How many of them ever got a true reason? The business you're considering buying likely has been equally clueless.

The worst thing that can happen is you find that neither employees nor customers have as deep a sense of loyalty to the business and the brand as you thought or hoped, and the next thing you know you're not only in business for yourself, but also by yourself.

Our business is really simple. When you look at a deal and its structure looks like an octopus or spider, just don't do it.

— Timothy Sloan, CFO of Wells Fargo

While each of these factors listed above may or may not be a concern, finding a deal on a great business for acquisition that fits you well is difficult. First, such deals are not easy to find. Second, there are a lot of people looking. If it is a good deal, you will rarely be the only one negotiating for the business. If you are alone and nobody else is looking to buy it, ask yourself why.

Below is a chart of key considerations when purchasing an existing business. Yes, it can be done. Yes, it can be challenging to find the needle in the haystack.

Industry
- Highly fragmented
- Stable / low cyclicaility
- Growing at > 2x GDP
- Low external risk factors (i.e. regulation, technology obsolescence, etc.)

Company
- High percentage of recurring / repeatable revenue
- Track record of consistent profitability
- Diverse customer base
- Strong middle management

Financial
- Revenue between $5 - 50 million
- Stable cash flows of at least $1 million
- EBITDA margins > 10%
- Low capex and working capital requirements

Context
- Owner seeking liquidity and wanting to retire / transition out of daily operations
- No succession plan in place
- Company in need of additional management, capital and board expertise to capture groth opportunities

Now let's talk about franchising, which can often serve as a better option for entrepreneurs and investors.

Because we have already discussed the pros and cons of franchising in the previous chapter, we won't go into the same level of detail. The things you want as a result of buying an existing business (proven model, roadmap, learnings, many items already in place, etc) can also be derived from purchasing a franchise... but the cost of entry is lower on average as you are not paying a multiple of past earnings. In addition, you have the support of the franchisor and other franchisees as well as leverage in buying power, large data sets for marketing, partners in innovation, the potential of a more profitable future exit and more.

Before we go too much further, let's talk about a paradigm shift in your thinking. When you purchase the rights to a franchise, rather than being a buyer of a business, from day one you are setting yourself up to one day be a seller of the business. This is the seat you want to be in! Nobody owns a business forever. Life is terminal, and therefore so is business ownership. There are two ways to go out: close the business, which terminates all revenue, or sell the business, which can result in revenue for your retirement and for your legacy. Start with the mindset of a legacy planner and buy a business with the full awareness that someday you will want to sell it. Build it into a business that a future buyer would love to acquire!

It is worth stating again that a franchise owner who sells their business tends to average a 50% higher exit price than that of other businesses in their industry. A franchise, in other words, is a better store of value.

When it comes to entrepreneurship through acquisition, many of my clients see the trade off of getting started at a lower price with a more proven entity even if it requires putting in a little bit of effort out of the gate as a better alternative to paying out the profit of the past several years of an operating business that lacks support beyond its current team and all of the inherent risks we mentioned above.

Three chapters in, you may be shaken a bit; that's good, it means you're learning. If this book is causing you to rethink your approach to entrepreneurship, that's alright. At the very least, you are getting a chance to reexamine what you thought you knew. But whatever you do, don't give up on dreaming. Hang in there. I trust you'll love where this is heading.

Twenty years from now, you will be more disappointed by the things that you didn't do than by the ones you did do, so throw off the bowlines, sail away from safe harbor, catch the trade winds in your sails.
— Mark Twain

The Franchise Landscape and Ownership Roles

"Everybody trades time for money. Even the entrepreneur. The only difference is, people in successful businesses trade their time for more money."
- Danny Iny in *Inc. Magazine*

There are several different ways to approach the role of ownership within a franchise business. Roughly half of my clients are looking to get into business as the 'owner/operator', meaning that they will be engaged in the business on a day-to-day level. The other half come to us looking for an opportunity where they can leverage valuable skills, relationships, and capital outside of managing a business' operations day-to-day. This latter role has various names but is commonly referred to as an 'executive', 'semi-passive', or 'semi-absentee' model.

Before we look at the two basic approaches and what would serve you best as an owner, it pays to know what the franchisors think. Do franchisors prefer to have the owners engaged in the business on a day-to-day basis? How do they like the executive model?

Most brands would love to have the owner serve as the operator because they know that nobody has buy-in like the owner does, nobody else has the same skin in the game. However, they also want the very best people to join their system and they know that these motivated and passionate all-stars often have their hands in other initiatives. Some franchises do require the owner to serve as operator and they will be clear about this upfront. From a high level, I would estimate that roughly 10% to 15% of non-food franchises we have selected to work with have this requirement. This leaves a vast majority that allow you to own a business but not serve in the role of day-to-day manager.

Let's examine the owner/operator role first.

What is an owner-operator? In this role, the owner has typically chosen to leave their current 9-to-5 day job and focus the majority of their personal work time and energy on building a team and overseeing their day-to-day activities as the General Manager or President of the business. To be more specific, depending on what is applicable to the particular functioning of the business, their day-to-day activities may include: 1) hiring and managing the team; 2) overseeing marketing efforts with the franchisor's home office team and potentially an outside marketing vendor; 3) meeting with clients and running appointments; 4) ordering inventory; 5) representing the brand by networking at groups like BNI (Business Networking International) and by getting involved in the Chamber of Commerce or other relevant groups; and 6) managing the books or working with a vendor to do so. In short, they will do anything and everything that goes into running a business. While it's perfectly fine to take on a franchise as an owner-operator, especially if you have a feeling that you are going to love what you do, not everyone comes to franchising looking to run the business. We'll leave the owner-operator for now, as it is fairly straightforward, and look at the other side of the coin.

I often talk about the concept of 'Franchising as an asset class'. Franchising can serve as an alternative investment vehicle for those looking to diversify their asset portfolio. This is attractive especially for those that want to have some level of involvement with their portfolio, although not necessarily the day-to-day, hands-on kind of involvement. Therefore, the other half of my clients fall into a second category of engagement that is not day-to-day, referred to earlier as the executive model.

Both of these roles involve more interaction with the investment than taking your money to a financial planner and investing it in a 401(k) for your retirement, but they don't always require as much involvement as many people think.

This flies in the face of the idea that purchasing a franchise equates to buying yourself a job. When you purchase a franchise, it is good to remember that you are building an asset and that you also receive the side benefit of expense deductions along the way. This is what we previously discussed as the trifecta.

Many executive model owners utilize their background, interests, and networks to lean into their High Payoff Activities, often referred to as "HPAs". This is a term my former business coach, Jack Daly, taught me. Essentially, you play to your strengths, where you get the most return for the time you are able to invest and then delegate everything else.

For example, if you have a background in accounting and have been breeding dogs as a hobby for forty years, a mobile dog grooming business could quickly tap an existing network of veterinarians, kennel clubs and dog owners who have purchased your puppies, etc., and while someone else can do the work of dog grooming in the truck, you're tapping your network for new client accounts and using your background in accounting to pay close attention to the bottom line. As you continue to read, begin to think about your networks, even in your hobbies and personal life.

I have personally adopted the referral network/HPA thinking with the businesses in which I have invested. For instance, I know a lot of builders, property managers, and other potential referral partners for our Driveway Company franchise in Atlanta. My reaching out and making these connections increases our lead flow and is a value-add to business. This is one of the key ways I can play to my HPAs in the limited time I give to the business each week. This networking supports our team in more significant ways than my overseeing worksites or interviewing new crews of labor. (In fact, I have never been on one of our job sites)!

Many people who are exploring the purchase of a franchise are already business owners. Some of them own existing businesses which are franchises and some own businesses which are not. They come to us looking to expand their portfolio of business investments through either adding in a complementary business or a diversifying business. This doesn't mean that you have to have previous experience as a business owner, and it doesn't mean you have to own multiple businesses. There may be a little more to learn - primarily around mindset, but it can be done. You might be surprised at how many of your neighbors also own a business. It isn't a foreign concept!

Here's an example of a complementary business purchase: a recent client of ours, Justin L. in the Atlanta area, had built up a sizable real estate brokerage practice and chose to buy into a property management franchise that would serve as a turnkey adjacent service, leveraging his relationships, lead flow, and team members within the real estate industry. He can sell a ten-unit apartment complex to an investor and turn around and manage it for them at signing. In this way, the apartment building investor or owner can also become a semi-absentee owner. Our client considered starting a property management business from scratch, but as soon as he was exposed to training, systems, and the reputation of the franchise, it quickly became a no-brainer for him. He set up one of his key employees to run the initiative and when we checked in with them recently, he couldn't be happier about his decision.

An example of a diversifying business purchase includes this one: we recently helped our client, John B. in Rochester, NY, purchase a one-stop shop garage renovation business earlier this year. Our client was a lifelong pharmacist that had started to get a side hustle going a few years back as he purchased FedEx routes. After building it to 26 trucks, he decided it was time to set the pharmaceutical practice to the side. Rather than looking at opportunities that could complement the FedEx business, he came to us with a desire to explore home services opportunities. We walked through roughly a dozen different niches he felt he could see himself addressing in his local market, and he narrowed it down to garage renovations. We then looked at three opportunities within this space to determine the best fit. Similar to our broker/property manager client, he is thrilled with his new purchase

22

and plans to expand his portfolio of business investments further once he stands up this second investment.

Please do not be discouraged if you feel that you don't have a strong local network, have an existing business to leverage, or have experience of running a business already. While these items can be helpful, they are by no means a necessity!

With the excess cash on the sidelines and lack of great investment options elsewhere, more and more people are turning to investing in businesses for the very first time in their lives. The idea of taking on an executive role and jumping on a touch base call with the team each week is appealing and allows executives to leverage their backgrounds to coach or mentor their managers. In this role, executives can derive a personal sense of fulfillment as they draw on their past experiences and groom the next generation for success.

In my experience, the executive owner will be heavily involved in 1) profit-and-loss management; 2) strategy; 3) managing the manager; 4) scaling the business through rolling out new territories or locations; and as their success grows, 5) adding additional businesses to their portfolio. These are all things that an owner-operator would do for his or her business as well, on top of the other responsibilities previously mentioned.

Roughly half of our clients that opt for this model look to bring on a strong General Manager to run the day-to-day operations while they focus on leading the GM and leaning into areas in which they can best serve the business. Our clients love that, with the executive model, they are not alone in overseeing the business. They also have the franchisor and the franchisor's team watching the business and supporting the GM along the way. This is another huge advantage that franchising offers to these semi-absentee owners.

While the executive model certainly looks great on paper, finding a good general manager can be daunting. If you don't have prior experience with a particular a candidate, you may have to cycle through more than one to find the right one. Think about your own personality: do you have the guts to fire someone if they're not running the business to your liking and are unable to course-correct in a short amount of time? If you don't want to cycle through GMs until you find a good one, this may require a slower, more thorough process of hiring; taking your time may be worth it in many cases.

We'll discuss the idea of a hybrid model more in depth later on, but for now, we'll just mention that a great way to find a great GM could include working as the owner-operator at first and seeing which one of your employees has good chemistry with you, shows the initiative, responsibility, and other characteristics you would want in a GM before promoting them and stepping into the Executive role. Of course, many, if not most, do not have the bandwidth to be active in this capacity - even at the onset.

Again, working in the business early on is not a necessity. We have many case studies of client successes in finding general managers and aligning interests with them through compensation packages that include items such as profit sharing and/or equity. We have taken the learnings and best practices from all of our clients and have now incorporated these principles into the value-add advice that we provide to our clients. We also recently launched a partnership with a national recruitment firm that will assist our clients in identifying and vetting key talent. This will serve as a game-changer for many!

If you have identified and hired a good general manager, you can really set them up to be the franchisee for all intents and purposes. For instance, with the Driveway Company franchise in Atlanta that I co-own, we have a manager, Andrew, who not only runs the day-to-day operation, but also serves as the liaison with the franchisor. Before joining our company, our manager was a C.P.A. for the previous five years. At age 27, he was antsy, felt stuck in a cubicle, and wanted to get out and work with people and build something.

Andrew is loving life now! He went to training with the franchisor when we first started, and we are letting him handle the day-to-day decision making. We get on the phone once a week to touch base, and we have several email and text exchanges throughout the week. He knows I'm here and ready to support him whenever he needs it, but I also give him the reins and autonomy to exercise his judgment in decision making. We also pull the team together once a month for a fun luncheon event and this is something we really look forward to, certainly not a chore. Business ownership can be fun. In fact, we recently sponsored a Nascar race in Atlanta, wrapping one of the cars with our branding. My family had the opportunity to spend time with the driver in our home the night before the big race and then joined him in the pit the day of the event!

With a GM in place, will everything be done exactly how you would do it? No; but if you have a good one, they will often surprise you with items for improvement that you never would have thought about, even if you were on the ground with the business every day. A good GM brings their own creativity and thoughtfulness to the work. Ultimately, if a GM can run the business in 80-85% alignment with the way you would, you should take it! Our GM at the Driveway Company, Andrew, is well above that mark. It made me think, "Let's go build some more!" (And that is exactly what we did, recently buying out two other franchisees' locations and expanding our footprint!)

It is important to note that Semi-Absentee or Executive leadership is not for the micro-manager! If you want to have your hands in everything, circle back to the idea of being the owner-operator. A lot of the decision making around choosing your best opportunity comes back to understanding yourself first.

Hybrid Approaches

There is a season for everything. Many new franchise owners have a desire to see their role evolve as they move forward. Here are a couple of ways that you may grow into the role you really want.

1. Beginning as an owner operator with the plan to bring on a GM later on. This allows the owner to really understand the business and its needs, as well as its path to scale. Their intent and desire is often to pull back their involvement in the business over time as they gradually adopt a role that includes more strategic vs. operational activities in support of the business. These owners desire to eventually work exclusively *on* the business, rather than *in* the business. They want to focus

25

on expansion, whether it be through rolling out additional locations or territories, or through acquiring another business, either complementary or diversifying, from the current one. It's not impossible to be strategic, to work on the business, or to seek out additional growth opportunities while serving as a true owner-operator, however, it wouldn't be accurate to say that you can give these things your full focus when you are running the day-to-day operations.

2. Others want to keep their current day job - at least for the time being. They may feel more secure relying on this primary source of family income until the franchise is really rolling, even though it is their dream to eventually run the business soup to nuts. In their approach, they begin by building and scaling the business on the side. Then, once the business is cash-flowing to the level they have targeted, they say goodbye to their boss and jump into the owner-operator role full time. I have seen this work very well, but I believe that it is contingent on them being willing to invest in a general manager who will serve as a business driver and get the wheels in motion prior to the owner jumping in full time.

One of the questions we frequently get asked is: 'How much time one should expect to invest in their business as an executive or semi-absentee owner'? In principle, the owner may eventually be able to put in as little as 5 hours a week. However, I encourage my clients to plan conservatively. If they anticipate working only 5 to 10 hours/week in the early going, they should probably round up and call it 10 to 15... or even 15 to 20. Realistically, nothing worth doing is easy... but in the end it is very doable and the rewards can be great.

Franchising provides a variety of industry opportunities, and by nature, some industries and their respective businesses are more conducive to the executive semi-absentee model than others. We will dig into this in our next chapter.

INDUSTRY OPPORTUNITIES

"There is only one success - to be able to spend your life in your own way."
- Christopher Morley

Why not food? Everybody eats, right? At a certain point in my career, I chose to niche my focus down to non-food franchises. I did it for several reasons:

1. Food franchises tend to require higher capital investments. In my view, this means that they carry a little more risk, especially if you are not in a highly recognizable national brand. Branding matters more in food than in many other categories. Regional brands, for instance, may have strong local followings, but plunking one down three states away from where the first ten stores are located is not very different from starting a mom-and-pop restaurant in terms of brand-name recognition. On the flip-side, the large national chains tend to already be saturated, meaning that your market likely already has one or two locations of a given concept with more in development... and the earlier players will have grabbed the premium locations.

2. Yes, everybody eats every day. However, food trends change over time and it is hard to predict the future. Think about

the success of food chains that did a good job of representing their products as healthy, farm-fresh, organic, and how some chains that never deviated from the greasy food that they sold began to struggle. Will the franchisor keep up with trends and will they be able to adapt in a large-scale way without going off-brand? You don't often see a franchise restaurant on a busy street corner closing, but when you do, it could have less to do with management and organization, and it could mean that the food they serve has gradually become less irrelevant to consumers without course corrections at the corporate kitchen.

3. In my humble opinion, there are simply easier ways to make money, many of which require less investment, often fewer employees, less weekends and evenings, and are void of supply chain/inventory & spoilage issues. If you could minimize risk and maximize your upside at the same time, why wouldn't you? This isn't about it being easier in terms of hard work, but easier really means smarter or more of a sure thing.

4. I don't personally have a background in food and if I were to include food within my focus areas, I would not be able to go in as deep and become an expert in other industries as each sector carries its own nuanced models and frameworks. For me, as a consultant, it benefits my clients if I focus on a strong, profitable, and highly desirable set of sectors. I would rather go deep vs. wide! Now, there are those who have a background in food or find that's where their heart is. They are willing to work through the challenges and they often experience good financial upside - especially as they build out a very large portfolio. I am very thankful for these individuals, as we certainly need them in the game!

5. Interestingly, I have found that 95% of my clients desire to be in industries outside of food. They feel similarly to me that while they could run food establishments, there are other

strong options that are often more compelling.

So what are people actually gravitating toward in the market for franchise opportunities? There are a few common threads that have emerged from my work with clients across North America in recent years. These include:

1. An interest in opportunities that may be deemed 'less sexy' and represent solid, understandable businesses. The core value that people seek here is simplicity. They want an area that operates in what is widely projected to be an ongoing market need and the franchisor knows how to fill it. Typically, the work isn't overly complicated with many moving parts - and it is certainly not trendy.

2. We have seen a desire for built-in resistance to disruption. Though nothing is ever completely predictable in life, for obvious reasons, we see a lot of interest in opportunities that are less likely to be disrupted by recessions, pandemics, or technology. Anything that can be seen as an essential service by the government and is more needs-based rather than tied to discretionary spending for the consumer is an attractive franchise these days.

One other thing that people want their businesses to resist is the invasiveness of mega-corporations. They want products and services that aren't likely to be threatened by a company such as Amazon who is capable of rolling out a brand-new service that instantly grabs huge chunks of market share across the country. Even though many franchisors do use technology - often as a differentiator, people are looking for something that is far less likely to be disrupted by the 'Amazons of the world'.

Again, it is nearly impossible to completely predict the future. For instance, which taxicab company saw Uber coming? How will blockchain and crypto currencies impact the next wave of how we do business? While the future is difficult to predict or foresee, the macro forces that are at work, based on recent global events, are transparent enough.

3. Another shift is the desire for a franchise that requires as few employees as possible while still delivering a high return on investment. Of course, this varies by owner as some individuals love leading large teams and even lean into their experience and skills in hiring, incentivizing, and retaining as a competitive advantage of theirs. That being said, I will point out that the desire for fewer employees has always been present to a degree, but I have certainly seen it rise in clients' ranking of importance in recent years. The fact is we have been working through the 'Great Resignation' (i.e. 'Great Reassessment') and more people have enjoyed working from home and being self-employed than ever before. At the same time, a variety of economic and political factors can make the job market tight; finding great employees when a great employee is in higher demand naturally means giving up more of your profit to your payroll to keep them happy and ensure their loyalty. The shift in how people want to be employed is mirrored by those who want to own a franchise.

Now, let's have some fun and talk specifics. What are some of the more popular industries today, along with examples of businesses contained within each?

1. Property services.

This category includes Business to Consumer (B2C) home services as well as

Business to Business (B2B) property services and also businesses that can serve both segments. I would say that hands down no other category broken out below has been hotter than property services in recent years for several reasons.

With property services, oftentimes, you can work remotely. If you do have to have a physical location, it isn't retail-based or customer-facing, rather more of a back end, small industrial space for equipment storage, team meetings, etc.

Not having a pricey lease has been attractive to many of our clients. Examples of property service businesses include recurring services such as property management or pool cleaning; but they can also offer one-time, bigger ticket items such as insulation, gutters, and driveway paving. People are loving the 'ServPro type models' of the world, where payment for the end customer is as transactional as an insurance claim. They also love niches such as roll-off dumpsters for construction sites, parking lot maintenance and line striping, etc. There are so many unique segments in highly fragmented industries in which you can bring a white-collar approach to managing traditionally blue collar businesses.

2. Health and Wellness.

There has never been so much interest in improving health and boosting immunity as there is currently. Fitness certainly took a breather during the Covid pandemic but has come back really strong ever since. All sorts of models and setups exist within the wide world of fitness, from big box gyms to boutique concepts and specialized services such as stretching and personal training.

An example of a differentiated model in the fitness space includes a placement we recently completed for a client: we helped our client, a PhD professor at a large university, get into a well-established concept that offers incredible technology that guides fitness programs for the market segment of customers over the age of 50. As you may have noticed, many in this demographic do not like the big box environment and, as a result, are largely uncatered to in the market.

Another non-fitness example in health and wellness includes this one: We had a client purchase ten locations of an IV drip business that was started in Rhode Island by two doctors. It has been on fire! The business is able to boost immunity at the cellular level, fight free radicals, and lower the occurrence of heavy metals in the body. This business model requires some educating of the public; however, this is cutting edge technology and our client has invested in the future of health care.

3. Automotive.

Auto has always contained a good slice of the non-food franchise pie, from Meineke, Maaco, car washes, and more. There are new models popping up every day, including an International waterless car wash that some of our clients have engaged in.

Electric cars are getting a lot of headlines these days but even fifteen years from now, studies show that fewer than 10-15% of cars on the road will be electric with the current average age of functional cars being twelve years. What this means for oil change businesses is that there is still a long runway ahead. We recently had a pair of clients purchase ten locations of an oil change franchise that specializes in constructing prefabricated buildings in unused parking spaces of a retailer's shopping center as a prime location for their kiosks. This franchisor has demonstrated strong financial financial results deriving from their model of great street visibility, convenience, and customer service.

4. Pets.

I have always said that people care about their kids, their pets, their homes and their health. They will continue to spend in all of these four areas, no matter what economic conditions. But pets? Pets are *really* special. The pet industry has never been more popular for franchisees to get into. Think about the sheer number of households with a pet in America: 90 million. That's 70% of all households, which creates an ongoing, insatiable need for caring services. And there are tons of options. From boarding and grooming to dog-walking and big box retail to veterinary care, there are franchise options at every price range and with a broad variety of setups.

We mentioned mobile dog grooming earlier when talking about how you might think through your personal contacts that would make getting a business rolling easier… again, if you love your pets, you might love running a business that helps other people take care of their pets, too.

The pet industry has niches as well. For instance, we recently helped a client begin franchising his service dog training business. He has carved out a great corner of the market and has built an amazing track record of success. He is seen as the best in the US at his craft and is now bringing other owners in on it as well.

5. Kids

Kids are almost as popular as pets. That sounds like a joke, but seriously, you raise a kid for eighteen years, or two or three kids for twenty to twenty-five years. One thing is for sure, people never stop making babies, again regardless of economic conditions, recessions, pandemics or anything else that's happening in the world. There will always be a pipeline of kids at all ages and that translates to a massive market for supporting services across the board. Some of the examples of franchises that serve this category include computer coding and development programming training, specialized day care, tutoring, youth sports, swim lessons, and more. One of the more popular franchise options in recent years is a martial arts concept with incredibly strong semi-absentee financials. The majority of owners in this one never thought they would be invested in a martial arts business, but they put their owner hat on and loved the characteristics of this franchise, such as 1) Strong monthly recurring revenue, 2) Few employees, no inventory, not open weekends, and 3) The feel-good community component of providing a service that both helps the anti-bullying cause and supports physical activity for kids who may not be as interested in team sports and therefore naturally gravitate to alternative sports options.

6. Older Population

In a social phenomenon that has been termed the "Silver Tsunami," there are more than ten thousand people turning sixty-five years old every day. No previous generation has ever had a stronger desire to age in place - i.e. in their own homes. The current wave of folks in this age group are often avoiding going to assisted living as long as they can, which opens up many more options to help them stay in the homes they love. Franchise offerings include plenty of options to support the

Silver Tsunami demographic. One example is in-home care, including those with specializations and areas of focus, like dementia.

This might sound like a subcategory of the Health and Fitness segment listed above, and in cases like in-home care, it is. However, it can also be a subcategory of Property Services. We work with franchise opportunities that provide offerings such as wheelchair ramps, stair lifts, bathroom retrofits, and more. These franchises specialize in allowing people to retain their mobility and accessibility throughout their home. We also partner with a great custom orthotics / insole company that uses 3D printing for a variety of foot issues and a nice benefit of this one is that Medicare recipients represent a large chunk of the customer base. Why not let the government pay your invoices? It's an easy sale.

7. Business to Business (B2B) services

B2B services can be a broad category. How about an example? We recently had a client, David S., in Indianapolis, purchase a business coaching franchise. He is now armed with all of the curriculum, assessments, marketing, training, and support and credibility to launch his practice vs. having to recreate the wheel on his own.

Here are a few other examples of franchises that offer services to support other businesses: there are franchises that provide bookkeeping and marketing; we love one business that promotes themselves as the "cost analyst expert". They analyze invoices and vendor agreements for small and medium size company owners and then leverage their collective buying power, forming agreements across a variety of vendors, and benchmarking providing clients with strong recommendations for cost-saving changes. Their business model includes a contract that allows them to participate in a percentage of the cost savings their customer gains for the next three years, but this revenue can sometimes be recurring as well. Often, by the time the three years' contract is up, the customer has grown their own business, purchased additional services, and is ready to begin another audit.

8. Other

From moveable storage (think PODS) to laundromats, mattress manufacturing to drug testing to salons, the options outside of food and lodging are extensive - and we keep adding to our list of possibilities as companies choose to franchise their businesses as a means to scale.

We are always working with the top development groups across the country to identify and vet the best options coming down the pipeline for our clients. For every franchise you can name, from Jiffy Lube to ServPro, there are dozens of franchises you've never heard about which have great financials and will fit your lifestyle and your existing skills and network. There really is a wide world outside of food!

Also, most opportunities never hit our clients' radar until they hear about them from us. This is why we love what we do: introducing clients to opportunities they never would have thought of on their own. We find that close to **ninety percent** of our clients actually end up selecting an opportunity that they never knew existed in an industry they had never considered!

FINANCIALS: FUNDING AND RETURNS

"If you want to be happy, set a goal that commands your thoughts, liberates your energy, and inspires your hopes."

- Andrew Carnegie

Perhaps by this point you're thinking, this all sounds wonderful, but how much can I really make? Why not invest further in completely passive areas such as the stock market or buy a lake house to enjoy and rent out?

I have found it to be eye opening for clients when they understand the returns that can be generated by many franchise systems in the market. Return potential very often surpasses what they could expect from other asset classes such as equities and most real estate investments. As a reminder, there are three tangible financial benefits of business ownership:

1. You have an ongoing cash flow.

2. You are able to write off expenses that a W2 employee cannot.

3. You are building an asset that should have exit value when you go to sell.

The exit value potential often gets overlooked when people think about franchise ownership, but rather than overlook it, we ought to consider this as a very important aspect. Just like any other business, the goal is to build up the revenue streams and the intrinsic qualities of the business so that a future buyer will be interested in paying you a premium to purchase it. Unless you plan to give the franchise to a family member, eventually you will want to sell the business.

It is worth mentioning, franchise businesses, on average, earn a higher resale price when compared with non-franchise businesses. This was proven out and reported on by a trio of researchers at the Marshall E. Rinker Sr. School of Business. "Our research supports the value of a franchise branded business," explained Dr. John P. Hayes, director of PBA's Titus Center for Franchising. "If two people operate the same type of business over a period of years and enjoy similar sales, the franchise business is more likely to sell at a higher price point. Business owners ought to be aware of that information in advance of launching a business." After examining 2,159 business resales over a 10-year period, the researchers found that franchise businesses sold at a 1.5X higher price than non-franchise businesses. Buyers of resales also clearly value the attractive proposition of franchises, *and* an existing franchise, proven and operating well in a certain geographical location, can be very enticing[1].

The 'Item 19'

Most franchise systems have an 'Item 19' breakout shown as one of the 23 items contained within their Franchise Disclosure Document, or FDD, which we will discuss in more depth in the next chapter. The Item 19 is a financial representation made by the brand, providing candidates with a view into the financial potential if they choose to invest. Every year the FDD and item 19 are updated with the latest information, including the prior year's financial performance across the system.

Some franchise systems will provide high level revenue figures for

---

1 John P. Hayes, CFE; David Smith; and Mary Kay Copeland, all members of the Rinker School of Business faculty, prepared a peer-reviewed study "Determinants Impacting Resale Premium Disparity when Selling a Small Business: A Predictive Non-Linear Approach." Fall 2021 issue of *The Journal of Business and Economic Studies*

a portion of their owners while others will go into great detail, showing all aspects of their owners' P&Ls - broken down either by performance quartiles, averages, medians or other breakouts. One franchise system we work with actually shows the P&Ls for all locations along with business-related metrics such as conversion rate and average sale. While they go above and beyond the norm (their Item 19 is twenty-four pages long!) I am beginning to see a greater level of detail in the majority of Item 19s I review.

Having spent a good portion of my career in the corporate world, I tend to think of the Item 19 as representing public information similar to the earnings releases for publicly traded companies (back in the day I was once responsible for writing these for our company!) Corporate entities' leadership teams have to be careful not to make representations of financial performance in private conversations that are not shared in publicly released materials. Any discrepancy could result in exposure to a lawsuit.

In the same way, franchisors and their teams have to be careful to not share results, estimates, or pro forma assumptions with candidates that are not included in their Item 19. It should be a red flag if someone from the franchise's corporate office said to you, "I know that Item 19 says [XYZ], but you can probably do even better."

While the franchisor is limited to sharing financial assumptions and direction based strictly on Item 19 representations, existing franchise owners within the given system are free to open their books to candidates and share any thoughts they have around financial performance during the validation process that a candidate goes through during the exploratory process (we will discuss this further in Chapter 8).

It is important to recognize that there are any number of minor variables in your market; and of course, you'll have to run your business well to achieve your targeted results. However, between the Item 19 and the validation feedback from other owners which we'll discuss later in the chapter on the franchise selection process, candidates should have a good grasp of potential financial performance—both top line and bottom line—before making the decision to move forward with a franchise purchase. This information is also invaluable when comparing multiple franchise opportunities from which to choose. Now, let's provide you with a better understanding on the actual numbers.

Profitability-wise, it is very common for franchises to deliver margins of 15-25% on the bottom line; that is, net margins, after all expenses have been paid. However, many of our recent client deals are with franchise systems that provide for net margin potential of close to 30%. In fact, four clients of ours that recently purchased the same property services franchise system in different markets around the US will hit an exact 30% bottom line margin if they perform average to the balance of the franchise system. However, based on the caliber of clients we work with, my guess is they will far surpass the average!

Now, while 30% may be the average bottom line for this system, the actual return on investment, or ROI, is actually much higher. This is because the average investment is roughly $200k and the average revenue is $1.8M. If you do the math, this shakes out to $540k (30% of $1.8M) / $200k = 270% return. Of course, the business will be ongoing so the return will actually be much greater than the one year snapshot. And, they will have a business that they can sell down the road. I certainly encourage my clients to plan conservatively, but when you look at models such as this, even a cautious financial projection can more than pay the bills.

We have had five clients recently buy into another fast growing, emerging brand that comes in at the 15% margin mark but with some very fast revenue ramp ups. Their first-year average revenue across their 30+ locations shows current owners are averaging $1.7M, with their second year at $2.7M, while the third year averages $3.9M! The initial investment on this one is also in the $200k range and we will leave the math to you for the total return on this one. So, what is the secret sauce to the fast ramp in this example? Very strong national account agreements provided to franchise owners by the franchisor.

Not all franchise systems reflect those kinds of revenues or that speed for ramping up, but we share this example to demonstrate that opportunities can deliver larger returns than many would expect. The total net earnings your franchise can make is not the only consideration, of course; a slower build or lower revenue percentage might be better for an individual based on their network or other factors we've discussed before.

Again, even with the Item 19 visibility and the feedback received during owner validation, we always encourage our clients to take a very conservative approach in their assumptions when they think through their pro forma planning. We like to steer toward opportunities that have enough meat on the bone that even if our clients were to underperform the average, again, an eventuality which is not likely given the types of individuals we work with, they would still be pleased with the overall return. This may mean decreasing your expectations vs. the Item 19 by five to seven percent, to be on the safe side. If you would still be satisfied with your results, the business may be a good fit all else considered.

Making half a million a year may sound great, but now you're wondering if it could be possible to get into a franchise at all. Perhaps you have more drive than cash. We'll discuss funding in a moment, but first let's talk about what the reality of the opportunity cost is. How much does it cost to invest in a franchise? It certainly varies. Roughly 75% of our client placements fall between $125,000 and $300,000, all in. Of the other 25%, about half are above this range and half are below.

The 'Item 7'

Every franchise system has an Item 7 within their FDD. This is represented as a range, inclusive of items such as the franchise fee, any equipment and/or vehicles needed, the build out of a retail space if the business is brick-and-mortar based, the startup costs, technology investments, and typical working capital estimates such as marketing expenses and personnel expenses for the first couple of months of operations. The range in the Item 7 can vary widely. For instance, in a non-retail, service-based business, the range may be shown as $90,000-$150,000. The largest variable in this type of business may be whether an owner chooses to purchase the initial vehicle (for example, a truck or delivery van) with cash, finance it, or lease it.

The one-time, up front franchise fee for one location or territory (defined oftentimes by population or number of addressable businesses or addressable houses with an income of at least $X depending on the type of business) is typically $49,000, give or take $5,000. There are some variations in franchise fees. However, I would estimate that 75% of the businesses you would look at fall into this range, from $44,000 to $54,000. Don't be surprised if this number is increased by ten to fifteen percent within even a few years after publication of this book due to inflation. Even so, the point stands that three quarters of the opportunities will be in a similar price range; after all, the franchisors are competing with one another for new owners.

Discounts of $10,000 to $20,000 are typically provided for additional or subsequent location purchases, so it is very common for owners to purchase three or more locations out of the gate, locking up the geography for an entire region for future development.

So what are the variables that impact the investment level of a franchise? The most common 'big hitters' would be 1) whether the business is brick-and-mortar (retail) based, requiring a build out and property lease; 2) whether the business is capital-heavy (think large, industrial equipment); and 3) how much paid marketing and advertising is required to drive the business out of the gate to ramp at the desired speed.

We have done deals for clients that have been as low as $65,000 all-in, however, the $125k-300k range is a good rule of thumb for the vast number of opportunities we consider to be the most attractive in the market right now.

Funding the franchise

How can a franchise be purchased and funded? There are some solid funding vehicles for franchises. In our experience, about one third of our clients self-fund their purchase, another third use Small Business Administration (SBA) loans, and the final third use a variety or combination of self-directed retirement accounts, portfolio loans, friends/family/equity partners or Home Equity Lines of Credit (HELOCs).

For those using SBA loans, most are using versions that require cash infusion of 20-30%. There are a few hurdles to jump through, but we have a great partner that helps our clients navigate the process, teeing them up with franchise friendly lending institutions at the end.

Given the current, lower rate borrowing environment (from a historical lending standpoint), many of our clients have tapped into the equity of their homes, using HELOCs for their initial funding.

As interest rates go up and down, the methods used for funding may change. If a candidate has strong holdings in non-retirement brokerage accounts, they can borrow against these in a fashion not too dissimilar from a line of credit and this is referred to as a "portfolio loan". These can carry the lowest interest rate of any borrowing vehicle and can be used to leverage up to 70% of your brokerage portfolio. I personally use this as it is a no-brainer way of 'leveraging' and setting up an opportunity for true arbitrage.

Within franchising, the Roll-Over as Business Startup ('ROBS') program is also very popular. This allows someone to use their retirement account to purchase the franchise. There are some stipulations in the inner workings, such as establishing the business as a C-corporation and requiring certain upkeep practices on the account. However, given the lack of great opportunities for retirement funds in the public markets, this can be a great avenue for many - especially for those later in their careers.

Did you serve in the military? Veterans, because of the service they have put forward on behalf of our country, are highly valued within the franchise world. A small token of appreciation is shown to them through franchise fee discounts that can range from $5,000 to $10,000 and sometimes even more. As a side note, veterans often make great owners with their backgrounds of discipline, hard work, and executing against a 'playbook'!

There are many ways to fund a franchise purchase. Knowing the financial potential that many of the systems can deliver makes the initial investment much easier. As we said in the introduction, the returns delivered by a franchise business purchase can truly be eye opening when compared to the initial capital outlay!

Franchise Disclosure
Document and Legal

"Opening a franchise can be a great way to start a business. It can also be
overwhelming when you initially receive the Franchise Disclosure Document."
- Houston Barnes

One of the great things about franchising is that it possesses multiple avenues of providing potential buyers with a full picture of the purchase prior to signing a franchise agreement. In this chapter, we will dig deeper into the most important set of data points - those contained within the Franchise Disclosure Document (FDD).

The FDD can be overwhelming, but by the time you finish reading this chapter, you should have an increased comfort level when reviewing your next FDD. After all, thousands and possibly millions of other people, like you, have read through FDDs and found that they have helped them gain a strong understanding of every aspect of the respective business before purchasing. You can too!

First off, the FDD is not optional; if you are exploring a franchise opportunity, you will absolutely get a copy and have a chance to review it in detail. Franchise systems are regulated by the Federal Trade Commission (FTC) and are required to have an FDD. The FDD is a legal disclosure document that franchisors must share with individuals interested in buying a franchise as part of the pre-sale due diligence process.

The document contains information essential to potential franchisees that are on the verge of making a significant investment. In the past, you may have heard of a UFOC and if so, you're likely wondering why we're talking about the FDD rather than the UFOC. This is because the FDD was previously known as the Uniform Franchise Offering Circular (UFOC) before it was revised by the FTC, the country's consumer protection agency, in July 2007. According to the FTC, franchisors have an obligation to provide the franchisee candidate with the FDD at least 14 days before it needs to be signed or before any initial money is exchanged. The franchisee candidate has a right to a copy of the FDD after the franchisor has received their application and agreed to consider it.

The FDD outlines comprehensive information about the roles of both parties involved in the franchise—the franchisor and the franchisee—and is designed to enable the potential franchisee to make an informed decision about their investment into the business. The document lays out how the investment will work in practice for the potential franchisee, which is critical because a franchise is a unique type of investment and business. I believe it is important for my clients to know that the FDD is written by the franchisor's attorneys to be a relatively one-sided document. While it provides candidates with good visibility, it also serves the important role of protecting the franchisor down the road against the risk of possible lawsuits. It also serves to protect franchisees in that it gives the franchisor the ability to take action, if needed, with other franchisees that may have chosen to go well out of bounds, and as a result, are risking harm to the brand. As a franchise owner, you want to know that you are protected in this way!

The FDD is divided into 23 sections referred to as 'Items', and the potential franchisee must review each of them before signing.

What exactly is a franchise from a legal point of view? A franchise is a *license* that a party (the franchisee) acquires to allow them to have access to a business' (the franchisor's) proprietary knowledge, processes, and trademarks. This gives the franchisee the ability to sell a product or provide a service under the business' name. In exchange for gaining the rights to the franchise, the franchisee usually pays the franchisor an initial start-up fee and then ongoing fees, often expressed as a percentage of revenue, or 'royalties'. It is worth noting, though, that buying a franchise will almost always entitle you to also benefit from the franchisor's training, support, and expanding brand power. It is like any other investment, though, in that there is no guarantee of success. Anyone who may entertain the idea of opening up a franchise should carefully weigh the pros and cons before doing so. The FDD is a critical source of information for that evaluation process—but it is not the only way to evaluate a franchisor.

I always encourage clients to have a franchise attorney review the FDD ahead of their purchase and I would say that roughly half of my clients choose to do so. The objective of the review is twofold. First, the attorney checks to ensure there are no one-off clauses that are atypical to most franchise systems they have reviewed in the past. If there are, they may not be a deal-breaker, but they can often necessitate some discussion and/or clarification. The second reason is to review the document with the candidate to ensure the candidate has a good understanding of the contents.

The candidate does not have to accept everything the franchisor says to be able to proceed. As part of the review, about a third of my clients will have an amendment to the FDD drawn up by the attorney that they ask the franchisor to agree to. It may pertain to their specific setup, market, or it could simply serve the purpose of providing clarification to language within the FDD that the franchisee and their attorney consider ambiguous. Assuming the requests are reasonable, most franchisors will agree to aspects of the amendment. However, having been a franchisor myself, I can assure you that the last thing a franchisor wants to do is show partiality to one owner that they are not showing to others for material items. Therefore, potential franchisees should consider exactly what it is they are requesting and whether the franchisor may see that as preferential treatment and, thus, not approve.

Now, let's get more specific about what is contained in the FDD. Below is a summary list of the 23 'Items':

1. **The franchisor and any parent companies, predecessors, and affiliates:** This section also establishes how long the franchisor has been operating.

2. **Business experience:** Item 2 outlines the experience of the executive team currently running the franchise system.

3. **Litigation:** Here, the FDD covers any pending legal actions, material actions, and prior actions against the franchise.

4. **Bankruptcy:** Any and all bankruptcies involving the franchise, its predecessors, and its affiliates must be disclosed in this section.

5. **Initial fees:** A franchisor must disclose any up-front fees to franchisees, as well as ongoing royalties.

6. **Other fees:** Undisclosed fees can be a source of dispute later on down the road, so a franchisor must be careful to reveal all charges to be fully transparent.

7. **Estimated initial investment:** The franchisee must be aware of what the low and high range of the initial investment can be, including an estimate of what amount is expected to be needed on hand for their working capital when the franchise opens.

8. **Restrictions on sources of products and services:** This section covers any required purchases of goods and services, in addition to disclosing any ownership or financial relationship between the franchise and required suppliers.

9. **Franchisee obligations:** In this section, the FDD lays out the franchisee's obligations - often in a reference table.

10. **Financing:** Outlines the conditions of any financing

arrangements between the franchisor and franchisee, as some franchise systems will offer financing to their owners.

11. **Franchisor's assistance: advertising, computer systems, and training:** Item 11 explains the pre-opening and ongoing assistance in a variety of business areas that the franchisee can expect from the franchisor.

12. **Territory:** The FTC makes no legal obligation or requirement upon the franchisor to give a franchisee any range or territory to do business, but this is the space where any geographical restrictions a franchisor is putting on the franchisee will be indicated.

13. **Trademarks:** Item 13 discloses the trademarks registered to the franchise.

14. **Patents, copyrights, and proprietary information:** This section discloses any and all of a franchise system's additional patents, copyrights, and other protected information not covered under the trademarks section.

15. **Obligation to participate in the actual operation of the franchise business:** Here, the FDD makes it explicit whether the franchise can be held as an arms-length investment (semi-absentee) or whether direct participation is required (owner-operator).

16. **Restrictions on what the franchisee may sell:** This covers whether only franchise approved goods and services can be sold, or, conversely, whether the owner may elect to add something for an additional revenue stream. For example, a fitness gym might restrict what types of merchandise and refreshments can be sold at the counter, or the owner may have the right to sell whatever they want.

17. **Renewal, termination, transfer, and dispute resolution:** Outlines the prescribed processes for all four of these issues

related to continuing, closing, or selling the business.

18. **Public figures:** Covers any person whose name or physical appearance is associated with the franchise. For example, this could be a particular celebrity who appears in franchise commercials. Obviously, this section, along with others, will be updated over time.

19. **Financial performance representations:** An optional space for a franchisor to estimate a franchise's potential performance, based on reasonable assumptions. The majority of franchises that we work with include an Item 19 and it is typically referenced more often than other Items during the exploration process with the exception of Item 7.

20. **Outlets and franchisee information:** In this section, the franchise statistics are disclosed regarding the number of company-owned outlets as well as the number of franchised outlets in operation for the prior three years.

21. **Financial statements:** A franchisor must provide three years of financial statements to the franchisee as part of the FDD. This includes balance sheets, statements of operations, owner's equity, and cash flows.

22. **Contracts:** Ready to sign? This is where the franchisor outlines the franchise agreement. It may also include financing agreements, product supply agreements, personal guarantees, software licensing agreements, and any other contracts specific to the franchise's situation.

23. **Receipts:** This is the final section of the FDD. Here, the franchisor will review the disclosure and business decisions outlined between the two parties and provide the franchisee with any additional information that hasn't been covered in the previous 22 sections.

That may seem like a lot, but much of it is straightforward. When discussing opportunities with clients, once we get to the point of examining FDDs together, much of our conversation tends to center around Item 7, the investment range; and Item 19, the financial performance representations as mentioned above. In other words, we try to get a really clear picture about what it's going to cost and how much you're likely to make, the two key features of any investment. These two sections are great data points for comparisons, as we touched on in the prior chapter. As we mentioned above, the balance of the FDD is certainly worth having an attorney go over with you as well.

National and State Filings

Occasionally, when beginning your franchise exploration process, you may have to wait for a brief period of time to engage with a particular franchise system to learn more.

No matter where a franchisor is headquartered and operates from, Franchise Disclosure Documents are required to be audited annually with new each year filings to remain up to date with the federal government as well as the state government in some cases. These filings typically take place in the first few months of a new fiscal year and may cause a franchise system to 'go dark' for a brief period of time, during which new locations cannot be sold while the filings are processed.

This 'dark' period has zero impact on existing owners. It simply impacts the timing of the brands to sell NEW locations in the state in the upcoming year.

In addition, there are 14 'Registration States' that, in addition to the Federal Franchise Laws, have state laws on the books that require franchisors to register their FDD with a local state regulator before offering or selling a franchise within the state. At the time of publication of this book, these states included California, Hawaii, Illinois, Indiana, Maryland, Michigan, Minnesota, New York, North Dakota, Rhode Island, South Dakota, Virginia, Washington, and Wisconsin.

As a result, franchise brands may delay offering ownership opportunities in these states, and if they choose to move forward, there will likely be a lag before candidates are able to engage in their respective discovery process. In general, you can expect that purchasing a franchise with an emerging brand may take a bit more time in these areas.

One closing thought - while the FDD can be intimidating and seem restrictive upon first review, it is important to understand the 'spirit' of the law and how it differs from the 'letter' of the law. Typically, a conversation with the respective franchisor behind the FDD will yield a better understanding as to the 'why' behind certain provisions as well as the likelihood of the provisions actually ever needing to be enforced.

In the next chapter, we will discuss how the exploration and discovery process works.

SELECTING A FRANCHISE

"I have found that when you begin evaluating 'Option A' vs. 'Option B,' and you start to take steps in the direction of one of the two, 'Option C' very often comes along out of left field. Activity breeds activity."

- Jon Ostenson

L anding the right opportunity amongst the roughly 4,000 franchise brands in North America requires a methodical, focused process. It can be easy to get overwhelmed by the volume of opportunities and end up getting stuck in the weeds. But there's hope at the end of that tunnel, and having a guide to help you through the maze can pay off in a number of ways.

At FranBridge, we have designed a streamlined process that has proven to be both highly efficient and effective. Components of our process are not 100% unique to others in the industry, but our overall approach and support is superior. This is largely due to our reach, industry relationships, deal volume, and vetting capability driven by our past experience working both sides of the table. I have personal experience as a franchisor and as a multi-brand franchisee and this has served my clients tremendously as we review different aspects of opportunities in relation to each other.

It is worth noting that working with FranBridge carries zero cost to our clients. We are compensated by franchisors on the back-end, and for the franchisors it is a sales and marketing expense, meaning that not a nickel is passed along to our clients in any fashion. If you were to seek out a franchise directly vs. working with us you would be paying the same franchise fee. Also, because our fees are fairly standardized across all of our franchisors, we are able to work with our clients without bias and without a conflict of interest.

Now that we have gotten that out of the way, how does the exploratory process work?

Get to Know You Phase

First, we spend some time getting to know our clients through a phone discussion. We ask some key questions to 1) Help our clients begin to think through the types of options and 2) Provide us with the information to narrow down the field of potential opportunities to those that will be the best match for our client's consideration.

Second, we have our clients complete a brief questionnaire that provides us with supplementary information to ensure we are focusing on the right industries, investment levels, and role/participation level of the candidate in the business. Imagine, for example, that a client tells us that they are sure they are not interested in an owner-operator model. We can then eliminate that 15% of franchisors who require the owner to be engaged full time in the business.

Selecting and Narrowing Options Phase

1. Next, using the information provided from our clients, along with the broad experience we've gained by observing what is currently resonating with similar candidates across the country, we spend about a week reviewing the availability of opportunities in the client's desired geographical location or market to build a portfolio of opportunities, typically between 6 and 10 in number, to review with the client.

   During this time, we also provide clients with additional resources, which can serve to not only educate them on franchising but also tee up additional ideas and preferences as they begin to get a feel for the landscape and the types of opportunities most popular with others who are walking in their shoes with similar backgrounds. For instance, what are other candidates with families doing?, What are others who want to get into health and wellness drawn to in the market?, What has proven to be a great fit for others with a B2B sales background?, etc.

2. One of our favorite steps is reviewing the specific opportunities with our clients as this is often when we see the light bulb turn on and the magic begins to happen! We typically use an online webinar format to walk through the characteristics of each of the six to ten opportunities - the business model, leadership, investment and return levels, stories from some of our other clients who have bought into the business, competitive advantages, market niche, pros and cons, and why we see it is a good match for the client's personal lifestyle, current financial situation, and future goals.

3. Narrowing down further: After our review meeting, our clients choose between two and four opportunities with which to take a 'next step'.

Next Step Phase

The next step involves us introducing the client to the respective franchisors and then our clients can schedule introduction calls with the franchisors at their convenience. The following steps in each franchisor's process usually include:

1. An introductory call in which the business and brand overview is provided.

2. A 'Unit Economics' call in which the business' financials are discussed in depth.

3. An FDD (Franchise Disclosure Document) review + a territory mapping review.

4. Franchisee Validation Calls and Franchisor Leadership Calls.

5. 'Discovery Day' or 'Confirmation Day'.

6. Awarding of a franchise (i.e. an offer to join the franchise system).

The process is designed to ensure that candidates have as much information as possible and can make an informed decision with eyes wide open.

To expand on the Validation Calls, these serve as an opportunity for candidates to speak with existing owners of the given franchise system, learning about their ramp up and the support they received from the franchisor, hearing how their financials have shaken out, etc. Were their projections too aggressive? Or were their results better than expected? Existing owners, unlike franchisors, are not limited in the financial representations they can make. They can be an open book - and a great source of information, on all sorts of topics.

Moving forward to the Discovery Day, what does this typically look like? The Discovery Day, also referred to as 'Confirmation Day' or 'Meet the Team Day' typically consists of a full day or a day and a half onsite visit at the franchisor's headquarters. The event usually kicks off with a dinner followed by an all-day session the following day. Presentations will be provided by the franchisor's team in areas such as training, marketing, and operations. Candidates really get to know the team that would be supporting them day in and day out. The franchisor will also get to know the candidates better to ensure there is a fit both ways. After the Discovery Day, if candidates are extended an offer to join the franchise system (referred to as the 'awarding of a franchise'), they will typically have a week or two to make a final decision.

When are candidates locked in and committed? Not until the end. They are able to drop out of the process with any of the franchise brands at any given time. It is very typical for a candidate to start out looking at three brands, drop one after an initial call or two, and then potentially bring back another opportunity for consideration as each call provides them with new thoughts and their thinking evolves. It can be an iterative approach. It's almost as if you're watching a scale with a basket on either side as it leans first one way and then to the other.

Even attending Discovery Day can be an eye-opening experience, after which prospective franchisees have second thoughts. There is no obligation to purchase a franchise, even at such a late phase in the game. That being said, I encourage clients not to attend Discovery Day unless they are at least 80% sure they will move forward with the opportunity should everything check out. The franchisor would agree with this approach.

Throughout the process

We check in with our clients every 7-10 days throughout the process, holding their hand and serving as a sounding board. We answer questions, help them compare opportunities, share perspectives, and assist them in introducing new opportunities to the mix if needed. Our clients' thinking always evolves as they go through the franchisor discussions, so sometimes we even bring in an additional couple of opportunities for consideration a few steps in. We also help our clients through introducing them to the best funding sources, recruitment resources, and a franchise attorney if desired. During the process, we also have conversations on our own with the franchisors, ensuring that our clients are getting everything they need and covering all bases.

Additionally, it is not uncommon that we go to bat in negotiating for our clients - either on components of the franchise agreement such as territory size expansions or positioning our clients against other candidates that are looking at the same brand in the same market. This is extremely common - taking place at least 40-50% of the time. It can be competitive out there and we always fight for our clients... (and we usually win)!

From start to finish, the exploratory process typically lasts 30-75 days from the initial introductory call with the franchisor, with the vast majority happening in the 45-60 days. It is important to note that after this process you are not expected to launch the business the very next day. Oftentimes I will have clients wait several months - even up to 9 months as they like to get their ducks in a row, make some initial hires, and attend the franchisor's training sessions at a time that fits within their overall schedule. As a side note, your day to day life never slows down when you attempt to carve out time to evaluate business opportunities!

Working with Franchise Sales Organizations

One thing worth mentioning is that many brands, especially 'emerging brands' or those early in their growth, will often use Franchise Sales Organizations (or 'FSO's).

These franchise development groups play an important role for growing brands in that they serve as the sales arm of the franchisor's organization and lead candidates through the discovery process. For all intents and purposes, these groups know the brands they represent as well, if not better, than an in-house resource would, because they are specialists. Note that the franchisor will still get involved in the process and will be the ultimate decision maker on each candidate. However, by using an FSO, they typically do not get involved until midway or later in the process.

I frequently encourage emerging franchisors to consider using one of the FSO groups as it allows the franchisor's headquarters staff to focus their time and efforts on supporting the newly onboarded franchisees, rather than spending most of their time trying to sell new locations. Many of the 'hottest' brands in recent years have been represented by a top notch FSO. We are fortunate to have strong relationships with all of the preeminent FSO groups in the United States. This allows us first crack at new opportunities coming down the pipeline before they hit everyone's radar and allows our clients to get in the door before their market is snatched up.

An important note - I often see clients either love or dislike their franchise brand or FSO sales rep (or 'developer' in franchise-speak). It can be hard to look beyond a personality clash with a developer and focus on the positives, or to see the negatives when the rep is such a lovely person, but I always remind my clients that their connection (or lack thereof) with the sales rep is a temporary relationship and that the most important relationship by far is with the actual franchisor and their leadership team. The franchisor and their staff will be the day-to-day support partner once the candidate enters the franchise system.

As mentioned above, even when an FSO organization is involved, candidates will still get ample time to connect with the franchisor. This takes place during the leadership calls, a one-on-one meeting prior to discovery day, and finally, at discovery day itself.

The discovery process is a new experience for most of our clients. Many people find it to be a really enjoyable experience. Of course, it is also easy to get a little overwhelmed, as I said before, life does not slow down to allow you to evaluate business opportunities. In fact, I have found that the world seems to conspire against people to increase their level of overall busyness and distractions during this time! I have had countless clients of ours receive job promotions, get hired for new jobs, or at a minimum, be given increased workloads as they walked through the process. Perhaps this is because the people who are most attracted to considering franchise ownership are open to growth; people who have this sort of growth mindset find advancement and increase waiting for them under every rock and behind every business opportunity meeting.

The exploratory process, overall, has proven to be tried and true, as evidenced by our results. By going through the process, you will look at businesses differently. You will develop a filter, or lens, through which you compare and contrast different types of opportunities; even gaining a more critical eye for the opportunities offered by advancing in your current job.

We believe that walking through the discovery with a consultant is a no-brainer. While you could go directly to brands' websites, you will quickly find that your eyes will glaze over. In addition, you will find that the brands always put their best foot forward with their marketing messaging. It is important to have a guide who knows the leadership teams behind the brands, what kind of momentum they have on the back end, and what trajectory of growth they are on. In addition, who is buying and why are they buying?

Having a guide who has walked in your shoes, that is, someone who has purchased franchises themselves and has even led franchise systems as a member of the C-suite team, is a highly valuable resource. Purchasing a franchise is a big decision, typically larger and more significant than buying a car, and you want to ensure you have the best expertise available at your fingertips when evaluating various opportunities and all facets contained within each.

Long-Term Strategies

"My biggest motivation? Just to keep challenging myself. I see life like one long University education that I never had - everyday I'm learning something new."
                                                            - Richard Branson

I n Stephen Covey's *7 Habits of Highly Successful People,* he encourages readers to "begin with the end in mind." This certainly applies to the strategies employed as you evaluate a franchise purchase. While life rarely works out in perfect unison with the plans you have drawn up, having a general direction that aligns with your long-term goals will shed insight for you on the best path forward.

Many of my clients tend to over-analyze their purchase decision because, frankly, they have more than enough data, which tempts them into getting caught up in the weeds. This is the double-edged sword of the readily available information provided in the franchise exploration process information such as the FDD, other franchisor-provided data points, and current franchisees' validation anecdotes - all of which we discussed in prior chapters. One of the most important things is to determine what the end goals are and then create strategies that are in harmony with that direction.

That being said, let's touch on several common strategies that I have seen my clients adopt. There are three basic approaches we will look at: Single-Brand Focus, Complementary Portfolio, and Diversified Portfolio.

Single Brand Focus

As the name suggests, the candidates who choose this strategy are looking to go deep with one brand, scaling through an expanded geographical area. For instance, I have had clients purchase the rights to as many as ten locations both in territories for service-based businesses as well as in traditional brick-and-mortar locations. Their desire is to really learn the brand inside and out, eat/sleep/breathe the business and milk it for all it is worth, across an entire portion of a state or within multiple metros.

While I have had clients, oftentimes as multi-investor partnerships, go for ten locations, it is much more common for those I work with to opt for three or four locations or territories out of the gate. Typically, they will begin operating in one or two of the locations they've purchased and focus their marketing efforts there. While they do have the right to serve all locations out of the gate, they want to keep their efforts focused and concentrated, expanding their marketing over time into the other territories they have purchased once they are comfortable working the system.

The speed or rate of expansion is usually discussed with the franchisor prior to making the purchase and we call this the 'development schedule'. The franchisor wants their brand in every location, but they understand the sensibility behind doing it one step at a time, too. They want the owners to be set up for success by not moving too quickly to expand.

Note that, while the geographical footprint in a multi-unit approach is most often contiguous, this is not always the case. I have had a handful of clients who have operated in multiple states - as many as six states at a time. While this can create some challenges, it can also maximize the opportunity. For instance, if the business lends itself to a certain type of market, such as a city neighborhood with a certain population density or within a region of particular economic or cultural demographics, it may require expanding to non-contiguous areas, assuming the operational capabilities can be put in place in a remote location.

Complementary Portfolio

As you would guess, this strategy involves the development of a collection, or portfolio, of businesses. Whether this is done via franchise businesses alone or through a mix of franchise and non-franchise opportunities, the goal is for all of the businesses to provide synergies to each other. Many of my clients have purchased brands, often multi-location, with the primary intention to scale and expand through the acquisition of additional, nearby businesses over time. I encourage them to only launch one franchise at a time with this strategy, as I have personally been involved in a two-brand launch myself and found that it spread our focus and efforts a little thinner than I would have liked. In hindsight, we should have given ourselves at least a six-month staggered start between launches. No matter how ambitious and energetic you may feel when you start, there is a point at which your extra work may produce diminishing returns. Pace yourself.

I have enjoyed seeing clients of mine come back and purchase additional businesses after successfully launching their first one. They have been able to bring their objectives embedded in this approach to fruition. They find opportunities for synergy, such as:

A. Reduced customer acquisition cost. For instance, if you already have a trusted and established customer relationship, being able to offer them an additional service that ties in or complements the first is a no-brainer and will not alienate the consumer. Reducing acquisition costs can really impact the bottom line in many businesses.

B. Economies of scale through shared resources. This can be in areas such as shared office space for administrative and finance work, a single employee answering the phone for multiple businesses, or on the front end with sales and marketing (as point A above suggests). As your small business grows, you will typically require fractional employees in administration, for example, your need may begin with a half-time position, then expand to three-quarters, and then eventually one-and-aquarter, and so on. Having the ability to have someone work on multiple businesses helps the owner level and adjust the workload and balance out an employee's involvement.

C. Opportunities for advancement. I have had clients who have become highly skilled at acquiring talent as a result of the career paths that they were able to offer candidates. If a new hire can see a path forward in which they have potential assignments and promotional opportunities across multiple businesses, this can be very attractive to them - and a competitive advantage to the owner of the businesses.

One client of mine has found that hiring employees in their mid-twenties in his organization, then watching them prove themselves and earn his trust, has provided a fertile recruitment pool for future general managers of businesses which are not yet on his radar. As these employees become ready for this type of role, he comes to us to guide him into the next opportunity that he can onboard, promoting and thus retaining these excellent workers. He recognizes that providing additional responsibility to them is something that will continue to challenge them and allow them to earn more for their often growing families over time.

Let's touch on another client example of a complementary approach. Our client, Lucas B., in Columbia, South Carolina, had built up several non-franchise businesses across multiple industries. He noticed that he had very strong connections and relationships with companies in the construction arena, in particular, where one of his businesses was involved. Together, we looked at a number of opportunities that could leverage these relationships.

Lucas realized that his ability to get out of the gate quickly on the front end, plus the infrastructure of a franchise system on the back-end, would set him up for strong success. And that is exactly what happened. Lucas purchased a multi-territory roll-off dumpster business and has since come back to purchase the rights to several additional locations. He is thriving - and having fun doing it!

Diversified Portfolio

Whether someone is looking to diversify intentionally, or simply has the ability to be opportunistic and flexible when an attractive option comes along, the diversified approach can provide great benefits.

While there may still be economies of scale and potential opportunities for advancement as we just discussed, the 'Diversified' approach likely has less front-end customer marketing crossovers as a benefit. However, one of the objectives of this approach often lies more in the potential of non-beta correlations (to use technical speak). For instance, if a particular industry was hit due to a worldwide pandemic, having ownership of businesses that fall outside of the industry, as well, can lead to possible offsets. An impact in one sector in which you own a business does not mean you have to struggle overall - if you are diversified.

That being said, I would say the greater desire toward diversification within franchising lies not in the risk mitigation side but rather in the expansion of exposure as well as personal interest. As a business owner, having variety on a day-to-day basis can be a great outlet for those who have other interests. As a business owner, you become aware of the things you like and don't like within your current business, and this leads you toward what to look for and avoid in the next opportunity as you continue to diversify.

Having multiple types of businesses can simply be more fun and interesting. Sometimes you don't know what you will be most passionate about until you get in the game and get exposed to life inside a business. Many clients that I work with have had successes in growing traditional, non-franchised, businesses in the past and they love the idea of now being able to start up new businesses via franchising rather quickly in comparison with their past experiences for all of the reasons we have covered in this book.

For another example of a diversification play, let's discuss our client Nathan B. Nathan is the largest franchisee of Two Men and a Truck Moving Service, operating in close to a dozen markets and generating north of $30M in annual revenue. Through his expansion efforts, Nathan has built up a solid organization underneath him. Nathan came to us several years ago with an interest in diversifying his ownership interests into other categories. We have since helped him get into multiple multi-territory purchases in the home services arena, as well as in the waste management space. In each case, Nathan inserted one of his young staff members that had earned his trust into the General Manager position and told them to go build a business from which they would both benefit.

Nathan's strategy has paid off well as his young GMs have quickly built and grown their respective businesses with Nathan's coaching from the sidelines and the support of the franchisor's operations teams. In each deal we have done together, Nathan has returned to purchase additional locations. Repeat purchases for expansion are one of our favorite forms of validation!

Owner-Operator

Don't forget that it is okay to have more modest ambitions. Not everyone is interested in owning multiple locations within one franchise, or complementary or diverse portfolios. Some prefer to build a business they can enjoy working in too, being involved in the day-to-day action for the sense of purpose they can derive from meeting customers' needs and investing in teams.

Others may prefer operating the business vs. working for a boss in the corporate world for the schedule flexibility, the financial rewards, and the sense of accomplishment of building something of their own.

Serving as an owner-operator does not mean that your lifestyle will necessarily dictate that you eat and breathe the business all the time. Having a single location or a few locations can be the long-term strategy that you leverage for the other things you want to do in life.

An example of an owner operator could be seen with our client, Sam L. in Los Angeles, CA. Sam was a former Silicon Valley executive that had moved from the Bay Area to LA to be closer to family. Sam came to us, interested in building a sizeable business, but he didn't know what that looked like and he didn't have a particular industry in mind. Through our process, we introduced him to a well-established commercial property services business that he quickly resonated with. While he was ok with the work itself, he saw the proven financial model and really appreciated the support and reputation of the franchisor. When Sam realized that he could leverage some of his past sales executives in the business, he felt that the opportunity was a no-brainer and jumped right in. While his background differs from his new business from an industry perspective, the management and leadership skills needed to be successful had been honed in his past. These were the most important keys to his future success within the support system of a strong franchisor.

While it is great to have a general sense for the strategic direction you want to grow, I encourage clients not to put too much pressure on themselves early on.

Your thinking, and to a degree, your strategy, will most certainly evolve as you go ahead with your plans, and you don't have to have it all figured out on day one. In fact, the majority of those we work with do not know what their long-term plans look like in any level of finite detail. They generally have a sense of what they would like to see when they look in the crystal ball, but they aren't certain which of these paths will be the best fit. I encourage people to stay open-minded, learn as they go, and to continue taking one step at a time. I have been at this long enough to know that there is this approach. I have seen the results over time.

Understanding the Franchisor's Perspective

"Business empires and dynasties are not built on day one, but they will never be built if you don't start on day one."

- Hrushee M. Sangani

Business owners reach out to me on a regular basis seeking guidance as to whether they should consider getting into franchising on the franchisor side. As they begin to learn that franchising includes many types of business outside the food-and-hospitality arena, the obvious question is to wonder whether their current business is 'franchise-able.' I love having these conversations and sharing my perspectives on the current franchise landscape, as well as helping them weigh the pros and cons of going down the franchise path.

As an involved member of the Entrepreneur's Organization, I have a steady stream of founders who are more often than not in an expansion mode of thinking and who are weighing options for the optimal path to growth. While I don't personally take companies through the franchising process, I have several great partners who do. They provide a soup-to-nuts approach that provides these would-be franchisors with a turnkey setup.

Drawing on my experience as a franchisor, as well as my time spent leading a firm that served as a franchise vendor, and of course as a franchisee myself, here are a few of my thoughts on the benefits of franchising your business, along with some other items for consideration.

From my perspective, franchising can be a great vehicle for scaling a business to new markets. To build a successful franchise brand, it is important to have a business with processes and systems that can be duplicated and replicated, and one that someone would want to invest in and run themselves. It goes without saying, but at its most basic roots, the business must have good revenue and profitable margins, as well as many of the other benefits we have discussed previously.

One of the best questions to ask yourself before you offer your business as a franchise opportunity is this: What makes your opportunity desirable? Obviously, it has to have a proven track record. The financials need to be attractive, relative to the resources and effort it would take someone to build and run it. However, it requires more than just solid financials. It needs to have a competitive advantage or niche in the market. This does not necessarily mean you have to have a patent or a highly proprietary element, though that is nice. It should, however, have at least some unique reason for existing. This could be a wealth of past marketing data that has steered your company toward a specialized approach to customer acquisition, which a new owner would benefit from. It could be a supply chain they could tap into, national accounts or strategic relationships they could draft off of, or a support team at the corporate office that they could leverage to scale much faster than on their own. Ideally, it needs to be an industry that is ripe for new entrants across a wide variety of markets, preferably in a growing segment of the economy.

No matter which of these things your company does best, you will need to have the systems and processes nailed down in-house so that when a consultant sends a candidate to you for discovery, they are impressed at how thorough your system is. When you compete for franchisees' attention, you're not necessarily competing against only companies in your own industry, rather you need to accept the paradigm shift of competing in the *Industry of Systems and Processes*.

Once you see that, you understand that when you begin to sell franchises, this is where you compete with everyone else, no matter what product or service they provide their end customers. You will want to be a very attractive opportunity for candidates that may be looking at opportunities across multiple industries.

If neither you (as the founder or CEO) nor your executive team has prior franchise experience, I always encourage founders to onboard some key resources with franchise experience on their resume, as franchising can be a unique animal. Primarily, franchising is dynamic in regards to the support needed for your newly minted franchisees. It is wise to have others on your team that truly understand the franchisor-franchisee dynamic.

So, what are some of the benefits of franchising your business as a way to scale it? Here are several:

1. You are using other people's money to expand rather than having to borrow or raise capital.

2. You get owners who know their local markets and have more skin in the game. As a business owner, you have always wanted your team to act as though they were owners. Through franchising you can actually accomplish this - literally!

3. You can get leverage over vendors through added volume. This can be in the traditional supply chain sense or it can be with service providers, such as outside marketing agencies. Almost anything your business has to buy can be acquired less expensively as you increase the volume.

4. You are building toward a nice exit. The bottom line is private equity LOVES franchising because of the model behind it. I receive calls daily from PE firms wanting my take on upstart franchises that they could potentially acquire. If you search Google for 'franchise acquisitions', you will see firsthand the massive, ongoing level of purchases taking place by those with deep pockets.

5. There is a true altruistic element to franchising your business. You are helping others successfully achieve the dream of business ownership, and you are indirectly creating a lot of jobs along the way!

But not everything is rosy, of course. So, what are the tradeoffs of franchising?

Some would argue that you may lose control of the brand. Theoretically, this is true, however, I believe this is often overblown. As long as you are careful to define the guardrails within your FDD and bring on good owners, you are not likely to not run into this possible issue in a serious way.

A more common challenge is that founders and CEOs don't go in eyes wide open on the franchisor side. As a franchisor, you need to understand that having owners personally purchase the opportunity to build a business under your umbrella will require you to provide them with strong, ongoing support. You will wake up one day and realize you have kids across North America who have placed high expectations on you. It is important that you keep them happy and playing well together!

Here are a few considerations from my experience:

1. Select your early owners even more carefully. I encourage new franchisors to not jump at the first candidates showing interest in their franchise opportunity. It is easy to get excited to find that someone is interested. Remember when your first girlfriend or boyfriend expressed an interest in you? It is easy to miss how that person might not be the right fit. But breaking up with any of your first five or ten franchisees can be much more of an issue than telling your seventeen-year-old crush that you are moving on.

   On the other hand, selecting the right owners—especially out of the gate paves the way for great long-term growth for the franchise system overall. The early owners will set the tone for the culture and will make a huge impact on the type of owners who will be attracted to the opportunity in the future.

Their financial performance will determine the data that gets built into Item 19 of the FDD and they will be the ones on the other end of franchisee validation calls during the exploratory process. These early pioneers will either be some of your best—or worst—salespeople. It is, therefore, wise to be highly selective and really vet the initial owners. It will take longer, but you will be glad you were patient!

2. Sales function: it is easy for new franchisors to get wrapped up in the time-consuming process of selling new locations. I believe it is wise for them to consider using an 'FSO' or Franchise Sales Organization, as previously discussed. There are a number of groups that do an outstanding job of representing you as if they were a member of your team. They know franchise recruitment and the best practices process-wise for the exploratory process. Let the FSOs do the time-consuming work of taking candidates through the first few steps of the development process, knowing that the vast majority of these will not eventually move forward with a purchase.

   You will still get involved in the development process and will make the ultimate call on a candidate, but using an FSO allows you to stay out of the process until it gets serious further down the line. This approach is better than a penny-wise/pound foolish attempt at mastering all things, which isn't doable. Your primary objective should be onboarding and supporting your newest owners and leading your support team in setting these new franchisees up for success.

3. Making money: Many would-be franchisors zero in on the franchisee fee and the potential royalty stream, in addition to the exit multiple they will one day enjoy. However, they need to understand how 'franchise economics' works in reality. From what I have seen, the initial franchise fee is quickly reduced and only a portion of it actually hits the bottom line of the franchisor. The fee gets consumed by marketing expenses as well as sales expenses, either through using consultants/

brokers or internal resources. Franchisors should view the franchise fee as a sales and marketing expense rather than as a large piece of their earnings potential.

The royalty can certainly become substantial over time as franchisors collect 5 to 8% of owners' gross revenues. Early on, however, the royalty stream will not add up to an enormous sum until the system is developed and growing steadily. In the early days, new franchisors use the majority of the royalties to pay for their home office support teams as they begin to work with the franchisees day in and day out. Think of the early royalty as a cover for administrative expenses.

So, where does an attractive franchisor bottom line spring from? I always encourage franchisors to think through opportunities to vertically integrate themselves. For instance, when I was at ShelfGenie, we had a manufacturing plant that developed the wooden boxes which became part of our customers' 'solution' for their pull-out cabinet shelving. We were able to take a healthy markup on the production of these custom boxes. This contributed to a very strong bottom-line for the company and an eventual exit.

Not every business will have an obvious area for vertical integration. But be creative. You can always find ways to tap into this strategy. These integration arrangements will naturally need to be disclosed to franchisees in the FDD. An example could be marking up advertising services. If advertising expenses for a franchisee with your preferred digital provider would normally cost $5,000/month, but you have been able to bulk buy based on all of the locations the provider is supporting, you may get a reduced rate to $3,500/month. Because you are overseeing the provider and working with them closely, so that each of your franchisees does not have to, you can justify adding in a management fee of $750/month per franchise location. In this scenario, everybody wins. The franchisee pays less than they would as a stand-alone business, plus they have less work in managing the provider. They also get the best insights of the provider, leading to optimization of ad spend as a result of the provider having visibility into large data sets across locations. As the franchisor, you win because you're creating a recurring income stream that drops to the bottom line and augments your royalties and other revenue sources. Also, you have successful franchisees with optimized marketing campaigns based on the support, data, etc.

Franchising isn't the right path to scale for every company. However, as more and more owners are waking up to both the variety of industry types getting involved as well as the benefits that are available through franchising, I am seeing more and more owners at least consider the option of becoming a franchisor as one of their potential strategies to scale.

We have been working with a number of businesses, in conjunction with our partners, that are going through the franchising process right now - from commercial cleaning to alternative medicine to flooring to yoga studios with even a few restaurants thrown in. We also recently helped a chiropractic clinic begin their franchisor journey and look forward to seeing the growth. The possibilities are endless, and at a minimum, I would strongly encourage you to consider whether franchising is the right choice for your business. In addition to the considerations shared above, we would be happy to engage in a discussion to help you consider the options.

For many companies out there, franchising just makes sense!

CONCLUSION

Throughout this book, we have discussed the fast-growing world of franchising in areas outside of food. We shed light on the different approaches to funding, the role of the owner within the business, and the longer-term strategies. We reviewed why franchising can be a better path to business ownership when compared to traditional startups and to purchases of existing businesses.

Certainly, there isn't a one size fits all model and everyone is wired differently. However, more and more would-be entrepreneurs and existing business owners are taking steps to uncover this vast universe of diverse opportunities, with many of them jumping in with two feet.

These new owners are recognizing the benefits that franchising can afford them, such as support systems, community, buying power, and a proven playbook. They are attracted to the ability of starting on 3rd base with a new venture vs. 1st base. They aren't looking to recreate the wheel or test product-market-fit on their own. Instead, they can step into a fully built vehicle, take the keys, and drive.

These entrepreneurs and investors recognize that one element of risk mitigation is that of being in business for themselves, but not by themselves. For instance, the vast majority of newly minted owners are now operating in a field in which they do not have experience on day 1.

However, they are able to bring their skill sets to the table and tag team with the franchisor, leveraging the franchisor's industry experience, systems, processes, and competitive advantages.

Many that are purchasing franchises today are doing it through the executive or semi-absentee model, continuing to spend the bulk of their time on their corporate job or the other businesses they were previously running. They are attracted to the dynamic of the franchisor's partnership in supporting their day-to-day General Manager that is running the business on their behalf. This is yet another benefit of franchising that startups and acquisitions of (non-franchised) businesses do not provide.

In this book, we hit on the legal aspects of franchising as well as the multiple approaches to funding. We provided a glimpse into the financial potential, which we continue to find eye opening for many of our clients. We covered the process of selecting the right franchise and how FranBridge supports its clients in doing so. A number of client examples were shared throughout the book. It was hard to pick and choose which ones to include as there are so many more that we would have liked to use as illustrations!

In summary, entrepreneurship is alive and well in North America. Recent events, such as the worldwide pandemic, have only increased the level of interest that we see in the market every day. Many are questioning the path they have been on and feel that it is time to make a change. They are coming to the conclusion that in a world of constant change both in the workplace and in their investment portfolios, they would like to have something in which they can have an additional degree of control - i.e., their own business.

As I shared in the opener, I firmly believe that there resides an entrepreneurial itch inside almost every one of us. Some ignore it and some kick the can down the road, looking for every possible excuse to stay on the sidelines. However, in my experience, for those that are willing to step out of their comfort zone and step into business ownership, the primary question they ask themselves in hindsight is 'why didn't I do that sooner'? In addition to my clients, this was my own experience as well.

I am so thankful that I personally have had the opportunity of running my own businesses. Since stepping away from the corporate world, I have never looked back. Not once. The freedom, autonomy, and financial rewards I have been blessed to achieve would never have reached the current level if I had continued to serve as a W-2 employee.

After leaving Corporate America, I had the opportunity to lead a great franchise system on the franchisor side and then step into ownership as a multi-brand franchisee. These experiences and the thousands of clients I have been so fortunate to work with have dramatically shaped my views on business ownership and investments. There is nothing that I love more now than opening the eyes of others to see the wide array of opportunities and approaches that exist.

Every day, more and more entrepreneurs and investors are discovering that non-food franchising is truly a better path to business ownership.

FranBridge Client Testimonials

"Simply put, Jon is an asset to every aspiring entrepreneur looking to take the leap and every business owner looking to scale. I'd say he is a natural, but the amount of effort and energy he puts into honing his craft is remarkable. He has a unique ability to sift through the noise, identify your primary objectives, and connect you with sound opportunities. His advice and counsel have put me on a trajectory to create generational wealth."

—Joe DeCantis (Jacksonville, FL)

"I was completely overwhelmed by the franchise process while I was searching on my own. When I found Franbridge on a podcast, I knew they were exactly the people I needed on my team. They helped me find a concept that was an absolutely perfect match for my skill set and experience. Since then, our company's growth has been explosive. I couldn't have done it without Franbridge!"

—Will Allen (Charlotte, NC)

"If you're seeking a trustworthy expert to help you navigate the world of franchising, look no further than Jon Ostenson. I don't know how Jon does it, but whenever any challenge would arise in my journey to find the right franchise fit, Jon would find the time to guide me through it, without exception. Buying a franchise can be a rollercoaster. Luckily for me, Jon was there for all the ups and downs, every twist and turn. I couldn't be happier with my decision to become a franchisee, and I can say without reservation that I couldn't have done it alone. Thank you, Jon!"

—Dave Sagalyn (Boston, MA)

"Working with Jon has been one of the best decisions made as we explored opportunities. The wealth of knowledge and experience coupled with the efforts made to not only get an understanding of our verticals of interest, but also placing intriguing brands/opportunities in front of our team for consideration, was invaluable. Our relationship with FranBridge is a highly revered partnership that we see as a long-term relationship to nurture."

—Darron Cooper (Baltimore, MD)

"Jon brought us such amazing options. We are thrilled to launch a side hustle in the health and wellness space. It will serve the community and generate a wonderful semi-passive cash flow for us. We appreciate all of your guidance in helping us land the perfect opportunity!"

—Kimberly Grant (Fayetteville, AR)

"I came to Jon looking for a franchise opportunity that complimented our existing real estate business. His very first suggestion ended up being a perfect fit. While we evaluated the opportunity, Jon's wisdom shined through his advice on whether a franchise was the way to go. I appreciated how he helped us clearly lay out the pros and cons, and make the best decision for our businesses. We ultimately made the decision to move forward with a property management franchise, and it was a great decision."

—Justin Landis (Atlanta, GA)

"I choose to work with Jon to introduce me to opportunities where he knew the teams and leadership well. He spent the time getting to know my strengths and goals and matched those with some really outstanding franchises. We worked together to evaluate my final two choices and now I am happy to say that I am a proud new owner of an awesome home services franchise. I would not be here without Jon to help guide me."

—John Bradley (Rochester, NY)

"FranBridge introduced me to a great roll-off dumpster business. I added this to my portfolio of companies and have since come back and bought additional locations. The business is on fire!"

—Lucas Bunch (Charleston, SC)

"FranBridge helped me every step of the way. There is nobody that could have supported us the way that they did with their deep industry knowledge and insights. We will be referring many more folks to Jon! Thank you!!!"

—Mary Beth Johnson (San Francisco, CA)

"I knew nothing about franchising before I met Jon. I have now acquired the franchise rights for 10 territories for an oil change business, 3 territories for a driveway repair company, and I'm franchising out my own flooring business. It goes without saying but Jon is well connected and he helps entrepreneurs take action!"

—Matt Wood (Atlanta, GA)

"When we got into a competitive situation with a rapidly expanding brand, Jon's experience and relationships made a HUGE difference and was a significant factor in us winning the territories we wanted. Because the franchisor respected Jon and the previous candidates that Jon brought to the table, the franchisor trusted Jon and his opinion of us. Not only that, but Jon was in a unique position (having worked with the brand previously) to help coach us (as first-time franchisees) up so we presented ourselves in the most positive way possible in a very competitive situation. Ultimately, the franchisor selected us and I know that Jon helped influence that decision in our favor. Because of our experience with Jon, I continue to stay in touch and look forward to hearing about new opportunities on the horizon."

—Albie Whitaker (Mobile, AL)

"Jon was great at understanding my background and presented a mix of franchise opportunities ranging from simple or complex B2B or B2C businesses to choose from. If anyone is looking into franchise opportunities and needs help in finding and evaluating opportunities, I'd highly recommend Jon and his team!"

—Sam Lee (Los Angeles, CA)

"Getting off on the right foot - Jon was incredibly supportive, knowledgeable, connected and transparent throughout the process. FranBridge and Jon work hard to vet opportunities that are a fit for each client's expertise and lifestyle, which are also among the top performing franchise businesses nationally, aligned with modern-day business values, along with the methods and digitally-centric processes for running companies in the decades ahead."

—Anthony Migliazzo (Westfield, NJ)

"Getting to know Jon both personally and professionally over the last year has been a fantastic experience. While he has become a great friend, he has also done wonders for me professionally. I have come to learn that Jon is one of the most connected people in the world of franchising. Since meeting Jon, he has helped me purchase into two successful franchise concepts (one where he also invested with me, putting his money where his mouth is) as well as help me begin the process of franchising one of my other businesses. If you are fortunate to get to know Jon, you will only be better for it!"

—Mike O'Connor (Seaside, FL)

"Deal is closed! 5 territories to start. Our goal is to purchase the remaining territories within several months. Thank you for all of the help!"

—Ken Winters and Sacha Jackson (Orange County, CA)

"Working with Jon with FranBridge was an exceptional experience. After having an initial conversation where any question can be asked, Jon came back to me with opportunities that are available, within my area, in my target investment range, and most importantly opportunities were all based on our initial conversation. Jon was well-educated on all of the opportunities. I did move forward, however, there was no pressure from FranBridge. Jon and I have kept in touch since I opened my business, and Jon has continued to provide insight about running a small business based on his experience. I plan to work with FranBridge again!"

—Greg Frist (Dallas, TX)

"I enjoyed working with The Franbridge Team. They helped me identify several successful franchises companies that fit our backgrounds, guided us through the process, supported our search, and finally helped us secure a successful franchise business. Thank you Franbridge!"

—Bryce Boyd (Atlanta, GA)

"I really appreciate all Jon has done. If he hadn't gone on White Coat Investor I wouldn't have ever known these opportunities existed!"

—Everett Brandon (Sunnyside, WA)

"Our experience with Jon was fantastic. Jon helped us identify opportunities that fit our needs and walked us through every step of the process. One of my favorite things about working with Jon is that he is always available for a quick call when I need to pick his brain. We look forward to working with Jon in the future on our next venture."

—Ad Boyle (Columbia, SC)

ABOUT THE AUTHOR

Jon Ostenson is in the top 1% of franchise consultants in the U.S. and is a frequent contributor on the topic of 'non-food franchising' for outlets such as Inc., Forbes, The Franchise Journal and Franchise Connect. Jon is a multi-brand franchisee and is grateful to have strong operators leading his ventures. As a result, he is able to commit over 90% of his time to serving as CEO of FranBridge Consulting where he helps others achieve their own dreams of freedom and wealth generation through business ownership.

Prior to FranBridge, Jon served as the President of ShelfGenie, a national franchise system with 200 locations. Before moving to ShelfGenie, Jon invested fifteen years in the corporate world, including a long tenure as Vice President of Sales for Carter's Inc., responsible for over $350M in annual sales. Jon began his career as a consultant with Accenture, often working internationally on behalf of clients. Jon is on the Board of Directors for the Entrepreneurs Organization (EO) and has BBA and MBA degrees from the University of Georgia. Jon lives in Atlanta where he and his wife, Jenny, have three children and are very active in the community.

Made in the USA
Columbia, SC
20 July 2023

20623518R00057